Making Law Review

Making Law Review

A Guide to the Write-On Competition

Second Edition
Revised Printing

Wes Henricksen

CAROLINA ACADEMIC PRESS

Durham, North Carolina

Making Law Review Second Edition, Revised Printing
ISBN: 978-1-5310-0810-9
The Library of Congress has cataloged the original 2017 printing as follows:

Library of Congress Cataloging-in-Publication Data

Names: Henricksen, Wes, author.
Title: Making law review : a guide to the write-on competition / Wes
  Henricksen.
Description: Second edition. | Durham, North Carolina : Carolina Academic
  Press, LLC, 2017. | Includes bibliographical references and index.
Identifiers: LCCN 2016059517 | ISBN 9781611636581 (alk. paper)
Subjects: LCSH: Legal composition. | Law students--United States--Handbooks,
  manuals, etc. | Law reviews--Competitions--United States.
Classification: LCC KF250 .H46 2017 | DDC 808.06/634--dc23
LC record available at https://lccn.loc.gov/2016059517

e-ISBN: 978-1-53100-555-9

Carolina Academic Press LLC
700 Kent Street
Durham, North Carolina 27701
Telephone (919) 489-7486
Fax (919) 493-5668
www.cap-press.com

Printed in the United States of America.

For Natalia

Contents

Acknowledgments   xi
Introduction   3

Chapter 1 · What Is the Law Review?   7
    A Little Historical Context   9
    Some Global Context   11
    Strange but True . . .   12

Chapter 2 · Should You Be on Law Review?   15
    Benefits   16
       1. Increased Employment Opportunities   16
       2. A Credential You Can Talk About   17
       3. Develop Relationships with Classmates and Professors   18
       4. Honing Your Lawyering Skills   19
       5. Unique Opportunity to Publish   19
       6. Potential Future Benefits — The Unknown Variable   20
    Drawbacks   21
       1. Time Consuming   21
       2. Tedious   22
       3. Obscure and Theoretical   23
       4. Law Review Backlash   24

Chapter 3 · Methods of Getting onto the Law Review   25
    Method #1: Grade-On   25
    Method #2: Write-On   26
    Method #3: Composite-On   27
    Method #4: Note-On   28
    Method #5: Walk-On   28

Chapter 4 · An Overview of the Write-On Competition   31
  The Main Assignment   31
  Casenote vs. Comment   33
  Casenotes   33
  Comments   35
  Other Possible Tasks   37

Chapter 5 · Preparing for the Write-On Competition   39
  Preparation Activity 1: Attend the Law Review
    Informational Meeting   39
  Preparation Activity 2: Clear Your Schedule   40
  Preparation Activity 3: Maximize Your Knowledge
    of the Bluebook   41
  Other Common Bluebooking Errors   43
  Bluebooking Quiz   45
  Preparation Activity 4: Read Old Submission Papers and
    Published Student Casenotes and Comments   47
  Casenote Excerpt   47
  Preparation Activity 5: Read the Papers You Wrote
    for Your First Year Legal Writing Course   51
  Preparation Activity 6: Create an Appropriate Atmosphere   51

Chapter 6 · Writing Your Submission Paper   53
  Step 1: Read and Re-Read the Instructions   54
    Important: Focus on the Prompt   55
  Step 2: Read All the Source Materials   56
  Step 3: Select a Claim   58
    a. Best Supported   59
    b. Most Original   59
    c. Politically Correct   60
    d. All Else Being Equal, Flip a Coin   60
  Step 4: Write a First Draft   60
    a. Follow the Instructions Regarding Structure and Format   61
    b. Make Effective Use of the Authorities   61
      i. Make sure that seemingly inapplicable
        authorities are not somehow useful
        to your argument   61

    ii. Differentiate between binding and
       persuasive authority   62

  c. Add Footnotes or Endnotes as You Write, and Use
    All the Space Allowed for Citations   63

  d. Keep Paragraphs Generally Short and Vary
    the Sentence Length   63

  e. Include Headings   64

  f. Use Active Voice   65

  g. Choose Your Words Carefully   66

    i. Prefer simple terms over complex ones   67

    ii. Use concrete words and phrases   67

    iii. Read your writing out loud   68

  h. Politically Correct (Again)   69

  i. Avoid Humor and Sarcasm   70

  j. Address Counterarguments   70

  k. Mind the Page Limit   71

Step 5: Do the Editing Exercise and Draft Your Personal
  Statement, if Your Competition Includes These   71

Step 6: Revise and Organize Your Paper   72

  a. Improve the Paper's Uniformity and Flow   73

  b. Make Sure Most Paragraphs Have a Topic Sentence   74

  c. Bridge the Paragraphs Together   74

  d. Make Sure There Is Consistency of Argument   76

  e. Avoid Redundancy   76

  f. Adhere to the Page Limit   77

  g. Save the Deleted Material   78

  h. Include an Introduction and a Conclusion   78

Step 7: Proofread   78

  a. Citations, Including Case Names   79

  b. Quotes   80

  c. Footnotes and Endnotes   80

  d. Style and Structure   81

  e. Your Paper's Title   82

Step 8: Maximize Your Paper's Aesthetic Quality   82

  a. Which Legal Document?   83

  b. Headings   84

    c. Body Text and Footnotes/Endnotes   84
    d. Use a Laser Printer   85
  Step 9: Do a Final Proofread Before Submitting Your Paper 85

Chapter 7 · The Editing Exercise   87
  1. Follow the Instructions   87
  2. If the Editing Exercise Is Paper-Based . . .   87
  3. If the Editing Exercise Is Computer-Based . . .   88
  4. Try to Find an Error in Every Footnote   88
  5. Don't Get Comfortable after Making a Few Edits   89
  6. Insert Notes If Allowed   89
  7. If You Don't Know It, Look It Up   90

Chapter 8 · The Personal Statement   91
  1. Follow the Directions   91
  2. Write Well   91
  3. Portray Yourself as Interesting and Likeable   92
  4. A Note on Specialty Journal Personal Statements   92
  5. Have Someone Review Your Personal Statement, If Allowed 93

Conclusion   95

Afterword   97

Appendix   101

Endnotes   105
  Introduction   105
  Chapter 1   105
  Chapter 2   107
  Chapter 3   107
  Chapter 4   108
  Chapter 5   109
  Chapter 6   109
  Afterword   110

Index   111

Acknowledgments

Many friends and colleagues of mine helped make this book a reality. I would first like to thank the following former law review members for generously contributing their time and knowledge to help make this book as complete and useful as possible: Janna Aginsky, Adam Brenneman, Marianne Hogan, and Charles Walsh. Their intelligent and thoughtful advice improved the book immeasurably. Many thanks, as well, to the numerous other law review members who took the time to discuss their law schools' write-on competitions with me. This book would have been incomplete without their assistance.

One law review member who deserves my highest praise is Patricia Blotzer. Her keen eye and attention to detail improved this Second Edition enormously.

I completed much of the initial research for *Making Law Review* at the law library at the Universidad de Puerto Rico in Río Piedras. I have many fond memories of walking up and down the aisles of bookshelves of the Biblioteca de Derecho, searching for this book or that law review volume. As happens to me in every library, I felt welcome, comfortable, and happy there. I owe UPR a big debt of gratitude.

I am greatly indebted, as well, to everyone at the Barry University School of Law whose support for this Second Edition helped make it possible. A few individuals there were particularly instrumental to this project: Dean Leticia Diaz and Professors Cathren Koehlert-Page, Brian Sites, Helia Hull, and Seema Mohapatra. Also, Katherine Sutcliffe-Lenart at Barry Law School and Professor Denitsa Mavrova Heinrich at the University of North Dakota School of Law each played an important role in the development of this Second Edition.

Three other individuals, each of them mentors of mine, also had a hand in breathing life into this book: Judge Robert H. Whaley, Magistrate Judge Bruce J. McGiverin, and Monty A. McIntyre. Their advice and example have been a guiding light for me in my own life and career.

I must also thank Benita Baird for the kindness and generosity she showed me while I was writing this book, and for lending me a hand when I very much needed it. Three recent colleagues of mine also deserve recognition here, not only for helping me out during the writing of this Second Edition, but also, and more importantly, for being great people to work with: Cherie Brodnax-Eaves, Tasha Rodney, and Jessie Torres.

I would also like to thank Bob Conrow for giving my manuscript a chance, Karen Clayton for helping me polish it up, Kelly Miller for the brilliant First Edition cover, and everyone else at Carolina Academic Press who helped make this book a reality. For their help with the Second Edition, I am also very grateful to Ryland Bowman, Charlsey Rutan, TJ Smithers, and Sara Hjelt.

And finally, my biggest thank-you goes to Natalia, my wife and my partner. How lucky I was when I first saw you all those years ago on the dance floor in Buenos Aires. I asked you to dance and you said yes. Everything that has happened since can be traced back to that simple and miraculous answer. Had you turned me down, I'd never have written this book.

Making Law Review

Introduction

Law review membership is one of the most coveted prizes in law school, and for good reason. Being on law review opens up more doors to law school graduates than any other single accomplishment. Whether you want to work at a law firm, serve as a judicial law clerk, or become a law professor, having the law review credential can determine whether or not you land the job you're seeking.

But although thousands of law students each year enter their respective school's write-on competition hoping to get on law review, few students adequately prepare for it. This is not surprising, since there are virtually no written materials dedicated to assisting law students in preparing for the competition. Because of this, most students simply sign up for the competition, pick up the packet of materials, and go to work on their submission paper without having an organized plan of how to tackle the write-on competition. This makes the job of those grading the submission papers very easy. Papers written by unprepared students are easy to spot and are quickly moved into the "no" pile.

I know all of this because I was once a law review editor and served as a write-on competition grader. In that capacity, I saw that the vast majority of the papers submitted were unorganized and poorly written—which are telltale signs of a lack of preparation. I decided to write this book so that the students who care the most about getting on law review have a resource to turn to in order to help them understand how the write-on competition works and how to master it.

My Story

During my first year of law school, I grew frustrated with my academic performance. Although I did all of my assigned readings, consistently participated in class discussions, and outlined tirelessly for each final exam, I still could not reach the top of my class. My grades were good, but not great, and I was desperate to bolster my résumé in any way possible in order to improve my chances of landing a summer associate position at a top-tier law firm.

I decided to participate in the write-on competition thinking that if I performed well, I might be able to make it onto one of my school's several journals. I did not even consider the possibility of getting onto the law review, figuring that my less-than-stellar grades precluded me from joining such a prestigious and stuffy publication.

Trying to improve my chances of making it onto a journal, I looked for printed or online competition preparation materials, but found none. The only information I came across was word-of-mouth rumors — mostly from law review members — on how the competition at my law school usually worked.

I was told by one law review member that the vast majority of the membership positions on my school's law review were chosen entirely, or at least mostly, based on candidates' first-year grades. That discouraging piece of news dashed any remaining hopes I may have had of making it onto the law review, since my grades were less-than-perfect. But being on one of the other journals, I thought to myself, wouldn't be so bad.

Based on the scraps of information I found regarding my law school's write-on competition, I mapped out a plan of how to maximize my potential of succeeding in the competition. When the write-on competition rolled around, I cleared my schedule, picked up the source materials, and went to work diligently drafting my submission paper, careful to follow the instructions to a T. I finished writing early, double-checked my work, and submitted my paper just before the deadline. Figuring my chances of making it onto any of my school's journals were slim to none, I promptly erased the competition from my mind and went to work for my first-year summer employer.

A few weeks later, to my amazement, I was invited to join the law review. I was excited to have been chosen, but one question lingered in my head: *How could I have gotten onto the law review with less-than-perfect grades?*

The answer to that question came to me one year later, while I was grading write-on submissions from the next year's class. As I pored over dozens of submission papers, I saw that most of them were unorganized and poorly written. It was easy to see that most of the authors of those papers had gone into the write-on competition unprepared.

As I read through sloppy paper after sloppy paper, a light switched on in my head, and I had — for lack of a better word — an epiphany: *I had made it onto the law review simply by being more prepared and organized than the other students.* This realization made me feel as though some valuable secret had just been revealed to me. I knew immediately that the strategy I had created to conquer my law school's write-on competition would be extremely beneficial for others preparing for their own law schools' competitions.

Following graduation, many doors opened for me as a result of my law review membership. For example, despite my less-than-perfect grades, I went straight to work for a top-tier California law firm. Then, after a year at the firm, I landed a judicial clerkship with a federal magistrate judge. Today, I am a law professor. For each of these positions I spent months preparing application materials, sent out hundreds of cover letters, résumés, and writing samples, and, in the end, got lucky. Moreover, for every job I've landed, I've been rejected from hundreds of others. So it is not as if my law review credential guaranteed me some dream career track. Nevertheless, I would have never even gotten an interview with any of the employers who *did* hire me without my law review credential. For me, at least, it has made all the difference.[1]

I am continually amazed at how much that submission paper I drafted during the write-on competition has helped open doors for me, and continues to open them, many years following graduation. I feel very fortunate to have been given the opportunity to enjoy this level of success, and I am eager to share it with others. Above all, I want to pass along the knowledge I picked up during my law review experience to help those hoping to make it onto their respective school's law review.

The Purpose of This Book

Students who familiarize themselves with the write-on competition and develop an organized plan of how to tackle it are much more likely to succeed in the competition and get onto their school's law review. This book is designed to help you become more familiar with how the competition works, how to prepare for it, and how to write a winning submission paper. In addition, it is designed to be as concise as possible, so as not to take up too much of your valuable time.

This book is also designed to be as comprehensive as possible. While preparing to write the book, I spoke with dozens of current and former law review members from a wide range of law schools in order to incorporate as many viewpoints as possible into this guide. As a result, the advice in this book should be useful for the vast majority of law students, even though the write-on competition varies from law school to law school.

Chapter 1

What Is the Law Review?

The primary function of the law review is to provide a vehicle for academic publishing in the field of law. The vast majority of law review articles are written by law professors, although it is not uncommon to find articles written by judges and practicing attorneys as well. Many law reviews also publish shorter articles written by law students, typically called "notes" or "comments."

Law review articles serve an important purpose in that they express the ideas of legal experts with regard to the direction the law should take in certain areas. Such writings have proven influential in the development of the law, and are occasionally cited as persuasive authority by the U.S. Supreme Court and other courts throughout the United States.

Almost every American law school publishes at least one law review, but most law schools have several. Generally, one law review at each school—sometimes referred to as the law school's "flagship" journal—publishes articles dealing with all areas of the law. This journal is normally named after the law school, such as the *Northwestern University Law Review* and the *UCLA Law Review*. Other journals publish only articles that focus on a specific area of law, such as the *Yale Journal of International Law*, the *Texas Journal of Women and the Law*, and the *Harvard Environmental Law Review*. These are known as "specialty law journals."

For the most part, the managing and editing of law reviews is handled by law students. The student editors

Note: Though the terms "law review" and "law journal" are theoretically synonymous, the former is most commonly used to refer to each law school's flagship journal. This book defers to the most common interpretation of the term, and therefore "law review" in this book will generally refer to flagship journals.

select which articles to publish, proofread them, cite-check them, and revise and polish them until they are of publishable quality. This delegation of responsibility to the hands of students is highly unique to the law school setting, since academic journals in other disciplines are almost always edited by professors.

Law review membership is highly sought after by law students, primarily because of the significant impact it has on their subsequent legal careers. Many federal judges, partners at prestigious law firms, and law professors were members of their school's law review. At schools with more than one journal, membership on the flagship journal is normally considered more prestigious than membership on a specialty law journal. In any case, membership on any journal can be a valuable credential when searching for summer or post-graduate employment.

Law review membership is usually divided into staff members and editors. On most journals, first-year members are considered "staff," while some or all second-year members serve as "editors." Second-year members also typically fill the senior editorial positions, including the coveted editor-in-chief position.

First-year staff members, called "associate editors" at some law reviews,[1] are normally expected to write a note or comment of publishable quality, although it may not actually be published. And despite the fact that most law reviews afford at least some staff members the opportunity to publish a note or comment, the number of student pieces published varies greatly from journal to journal. For example, the *Michigan Law Review* only publishes a small fraction of its staff members' student-written pieces,[2] whereas the *Washington Law Review* endeavors to publish a note or comment from nearly every one of its staff members.[3] In addition to writing their own note or comment, staff members edit and cite-check the articles that the law review publishes.

Second-year editors, by contrast, are normally responsible for reviewing and selecting articles for publication, managing the editing process, and assisting staff members in writing their notes and comments.

Some law reviews also offer their members the opportunity to participate in 'extracurricular' activities unrelated to publishing. For example, the *Suffolk University Law Review* runs a lecture series where students get a chance to listen and interact with highly respected judges, professors, practicing attorneys, public officials, and social activists. Many, if not most, law reviews and journals offer similar lecture events, typically referred to as symposia. However, other journals offer virtually no activities to their members outside of researching, writing, and editing.

In addition, depending on the law school, students may receive academic credit for their work on the law review, although some journals are entirely extracurricular.

A Little Historical Context

The law review as an institution has been an important feature at many of the country's top law schools for over a century. For example, the *University of Pennsylvania Law Review*, which is the oldest law review, has been published continuously since 1852.[4] Also among the oldest and most prestigious review publications are the *Harvard Law Review* (begun in 1887),[5] the *Yale Law Journal* (begun in 1891),[6] the *Columbia Law Review* (begun in 1901),[7] and the *Michigan Law Review* (begun in 1902).[8]

Early on, the law review struggled for acceptance by the legal establishment. In 1911, renowned Supreme Court Justice Oliver Wendell Holmes, Jr. dismissed law reviews in general as the "work of boys."[9]

But despite this and other early criticisms, the law review as an institution nonetheless gained popularity throughout the early twentieth century. As Professor Edwin N. Griswold wrote of the *Harvard Law Review*: "Some people are concerned that a major legal periodical in the United States is edited and managed by students. It is an unusual situation, but it started that way, and it developed mightily from its own strength."[10]

Following the lead of law schools such as Penn, Harvard, and Yale, many other law schools began establishing their own law reviews over the next few decades. The numbers speak for themselves. While in 1900 there were only seven law reviews,[11] that number had swelled to

33 by 1928.[12] Throughout the twentieth century, the number of law reviews nationwide ballooned. And nine years later, in 1937, the number of law reviews had jumped to 50.[13]

In addition to a flagship journal, many law schools have now established one or more specialty law journals. The result is an almost exponential increase in the number of specialty law journals nationwide. For example, the number of law journals specializing in intellectual property, technology, and art increased from two in 1980 to twenty-six in 2003.[14]

Combined, the number of law reviews and specialty law journals has ballooned in recent years. By 2005, the total number of such law journals had reached well above 500. This incredible growth is represented in the graph below.[15]

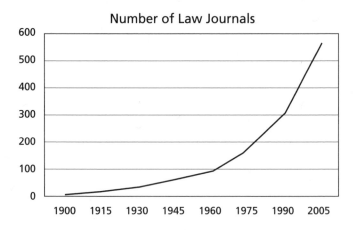

Scholars continue to debate the reasons why virtually every law school jumped on the law review bandwagon so quickly, but some clues to solving the mystery can be found in two inaugural law review issues. In 1917, the *Minnesota Law Review* opened its first issue by observing that, "The present position of the typical law school, as compared with the medical school, is discreditable to the former; its influence with the profession is not what it ought to be. The law review is one of the means by which the law school may make its influence … felt.…"[16] The editors of the *George Washington Law Review*, on the other hand, explained in their first issue that "Publication of a law review by any school is justified by the additional contributions to legal literature which it stimulates and the opportunities for better training to students which it affords."[17]

The ever expanding number of specialty law journals has similarly spawned much academic debate. Some observers question the usefulness of such journals[18] while others welcome the additional voices they add to the country's legal discourse.[19]

Whatever the reason for the law journal explosion, the fact of the matter is that over the past several decades, the law review and the other specialty journals have grown rapidly both in number and in importance. But through all the changes of the past few decades, the law review has maintained its spot at the top of the heap of law journal significance and influence.

Today, not only does virtually *every* law school have a law review, but it has in fact become an integral part of each host academic institution. It is no surprise, therefore, that law review membership has become one of the most highly sought after credentials by law students.

Some Global Context

The United States does not hold a monopoly over the law review industry. Law schools in both Canada and Australia publish student-run journals similar to those found at American law schools.

In Canada, some of the leading law reviews include the *University of Toronto Faculty of Law Review*, the *McGill Law Journal/Revue de droit de McGill*, the *Alberta Law Review*, the *University of British Columbia Law Review*, and the *Osgoode Hall Law Journal*.[20] These publications are among the most-cited law reviews by the Supreme Court of Canada, which also cites frequently from leading American law review articles.[21] Similar to their American counterparts, membership on these journals requires demanding time commitments, and many editors move on to top judicial clerkships or other highly competitive legal positions.[22]

In Australia, the leading student-edited peer-reviewed academic law reviews are the *Melbourne University Law Review* and the *Sydney Law Review*. However, the *Melbourne University Law Review* regularly outperforms *Sydney Law Review* on impact, citation in journals and cases, and combined rankings.[23] Nonetheless, these publications are among the most cited non-U.S. law reviews by U.S. journals.[24] The top international law journal in Australia is the *Melbourne Journal of International Law*, also a student-edited peer-reviewed academic law review.[25] Surprisingly, this specialty law journal is considered to be more influential and prestigious than most flagship law reviews in Australia.[26]

Strange but True ...

Despite the tedious and oftentimes dull nature of what law journals are and what they publish (recognizing, of course, that their purpose is not to entertain but to develop the law), there is another side to the legal academic publishing world: it is occasionally interesting. Really. Want proof? Read on.

Who says law review can't be funny? Although the *University of Pennsylvania Law Review* is the oldest and one of the most prestigious and influential law reviews in the country, it occasionally publishes humorous "asides." The most well known is *The Common Law Origins of the Infield Fly Rule*, 123 U. PA. L. REV. 1474 (1975). You don't believe me? Look it up! This and many, many other humorous law review publications are referenced in *A Compendium of Clever and Amusing Law Review Writings: An Idiosyncratic Bibliography of Miscellany With In Kind Annotations Intended as a Humorous Diversion for the Gentle Reader*, 51 DRAKE L. REV. 105 (2002).

It's published where? Surprisingly, the *Alaska Law Review*—a journal dedicated entirely to "legal issues affecting the state of Alaska"—is published not in Alaska, but at a law school that rarely ever sees snow. Although you would probably never have guessed it, the *Alaska Law Review* is actually published at Duke Law School in

Durham, North Carolina. You can check out their website to see for yourself at http://alr.law.duke.edu.

Don't like the law review article? Change it yourself! The *Wake Forest Law Review* at one time went *wiki*. The editors of that journal set up an online legal law review called the "*Wiki Legal Journal*," which could be accessed on a website they set up. The motivation behind this experimental online-only journal was to try "to overcome the plural author stigma and start a collaborative revolution in legal scholarship." The *Wiki Legal Journal* encouraged visitors to edit the articles posted on their website. Of course, some experiments work and some don't, and this one, apparently, fell squarely into the latter category. The *Wiki Legal Journal* is, as of this writing, no longer available and appears to have folded.

The World's Greatest Law Review Article? Really? Andrew J. McClurg wrote *The World's Greatest Law Review Article for Anyone Taking Life Too Seriously*, 81 OCT. A.B.A. J. 84 (1995). It is, in short, an over-the-top piece of satire of a law review article that begins: "This[1] is[2] the[3] world's[4] greatest[5] law[6] review[7] article.[8]" (All footnotes were in the original.) Its author, who also penned the books *1L of a Ride* and *The Lawyer Trip*, among others, went on to a long career in law teaching, which just goes to show that publishing just about anything—even a purposefully absurd parody—can help springboard aspiring academics into the ivory tower.

Chapter 2

Should You Be on Law Review?

You will be faced with very few significant choices during your first year of law school. You will not get to choose which classes to enroll in (since the first year law school curriculum is uniform nationwide, thanks to the ABA), which professors to take, or which section you'll be assigned to as an incoming law student. But you *will* face a very important decision toward the end of your first year of law school: whether to try and get onto the law review. You must make this decision during your first year because the write-on competition is normally only open to first year law students (commonly called "One-Ls"), and often presents the only opportunity to join the prestigious publication.

This decision will have repercussions many years into your professional career, and should not be taken lightly. Although law review membership brings with it unparalleled benefits, it also has some drawbacks. On the one hand, law review membership opens up innumerable doors to future employment, but on the other hand, it takes away valuable time from other activities that you may want to pursue instead.

Because you will have to live with this important decision not only for the rest of law school, but also—at least to some extent—for the rest of your life, it is important to consider the benefits of being on law review in order to determine whether it is worth it for you. Here are a few:

Benefits

1. Increased Employment Opportunities

Law students' plans for post-graduation are as diverse as the law students themselves. Many students plan on going into private practice while others aspire to serve as judicial law clerks, work for a government agency, or become law professors. However, almost all law students—including, presumably, yourself—have one employment goal in common: they want to have a job following graduation. And regardless of your particular employment goals, law review membership would be a very valuable credential on your résumé, and would set you apart from the competition as you commence your job hunt.

The great importance legal recruiters place on law review membership stems primarily from the assumption that if you made it onto law review, you have good grades and superior writing skills. But employers also value law review experience because it typically means you've had more practice proofreading, editing, and writing than non-law reviewers. These assumptions give law review members an advantage in the job hunt over non-members.

Another reason legal employers value the law review credential so highly is because it signals to them that the applicant can handle many tasks at once. Balancing law review duties with classes and extracurricular activities is quite difficult, and it presents a circumstance relatively equivalent to a lawyer handling several cases at once. Thus, the time-management skills learned as a law review member are somewhat transferable to law practice, and are often recognized as an asset by legal recruiters.

In addition to its value in the job market generally, there are certain legal jobs for which law review membership is almost a prerequisite. These include federal judicial clerkships, law professor positions,[1] and employment at top-tier law firms. If you aspire to land one of these jobs immediately following graduation, law review membership is nearly mandatory if you are not attending a top-ranked law school. Of course, it is still possible to land one of these jobs without being on law review, but it is significantly more difficult without the law review credential.

The law review credential, however, does lose much of its importance after a few years of post-graduation legal experience. Nevertheless, it is vitally important for landing your first job directly out of law school, particularly with respect to the positions mentioned above. At graduation day, there is very little to set you apart from your classmates in the eyes of prospective employers. So, adding law review to your résumé provides a unique opportunity to distinguish yourself from the competition.

2. A Credential You Can Talk About

Apart from law review, grades and class rank are probably the primary criteria upon which you will be assessed by prospective employers. However, one advantage that the law review credential holds over grades and class rank is that it is socially acceptable to bring up law review membership with potential employers. Whereas bringing up grades and class rank is a *faux pas* (i.e., it looks pretentious and snobby to try and sneak your GPA into a conversation), the law review credential can be safely worked into an interview or other conversation without breaking any social rules.

One student I spoke with in preparation to write this book described to me an on-campus interview she had had with a recruiter from a large law firm where she was able to bring up her law review credential. Her conversation with the interviewer went something like this:

Interviewer: "So, are you enjoying your second year of law school?"

Student: "Yes, I am. My classes are interesting and law review is keeping me very busy."

Interviewer: "Oh really? Tell me a little bit about what you do on law review."

Student: "Well, for one thing I'm writing an article regarding the impact of *Blakely v. Washington* on the federal sentencing guidelines. I'm also editing and cite-checking professional article submissions."

In this short exchange, the student was able to tactfully convey one of her most impressive credentials to the recruiter.

The ability to point out such a valuable credential is especially important in on-campus interviews, which typically last for only about fifteen to twenty minutes each. Every detail that can be worked into this short window of time is vital to your chances of landing a job with that employer.

3. Develop Relationships with Classmates and Professors

One of the most important benefits you will receive along with your law school education is the opportunity to meet and forge relationships with a large number of interesting and diverse people. Your time in law school is, ideally, an intellectually stimulating period in your life during which you learn not only from the casebooks, but also from your professors and classmates. In addition, the friendships and contacts you build during law school can enrich your personal and professional life throughout your career. As such, interaction with other students and professors is an important part of the law school experience.

One of the best ways to meet new people and develop relationships is to join an organization or club at your law school. Although there are many chances to do this (such as by becoming involved in student government or the ACLU), law review presents one of the best opportunities. For one thing, law review members generally get to know each other very well because they serve one or, more commonly, two years working, attending meetings, and socializing together. Under these circumstances, law review members often build strong bonds with one another and provide each other with personal and professional support for years following graduation.

In addition, law reviewers generally get the opportunity to interact with at least one professor on a more intimate level than do typical law students. This is because, while a law review member is writing her note or comment, she typically works with a faculty advisor who assists her in developing a topic, refining her argument, and polishing her written work. Since writing a note or comment takes several months' time and necessitates numerous drafts, it usually leads to extensive interaction between the student writer and her faculty advisor.

This relationship can be very important not only by helping the student improve her analytical and advocacy skills, but also by giving the law reviewer an authoritative voice on her behalf (usually in the form of a letter of recommendation) in regards to future pursuits, such as getting a job or going on to further graduate school. In short, law review presents its members with an exceptional opportunity to build relationships with classmates and professors.

4. Honing Your Lawyering Skills

Much of what you learn in law school is "throw-away" knowledge, acquired through rote memorization. Such knowledge includes, for example, the legal doctrines you learn in class, regurgitate on the final exam, and forget almost entirely two days later (if not *two hours* later). But some of the knowledge you acquire in law school will be instrumental in determining your success as a lawyer, such as an ability to effectively analyze legal issues, to conduct legal research, to edit for both style and substance, and to write articulately and persuasively. Your first year writing course should teach you the basics with regard to legal research, writing, and editing, and studying for your other classes should teach you the fundamentals of analytical reasoning.

However, law review membership offers an unparalleled opportunity to develop and fine-tune *all* of these skills. Writing a note or comment, editing other students' work, and proofreading and editing professional articles are all great opportunities to improve these essential skills. In addition, law review editing tasks teach students to be detail-oriented, an invaluable skill in legal writing. Thus, in many ways, the time a law reviewer dedicates to law review duties can be more valuable to her legal career than much of the time she spends studying for her classes. In sum, law review membership provides an excellent forum for honing your lawyering skills.

5. Unique Opportunity to Publish

All ABA-approved law schools require students to write a substantial legal article as part of their curriculum in order to qualify for graduation. Unfortunately for students, the vast majority of these articles are never published. But law review membership provides a unique opportunity to get a great benefit out of something that you, as a law student, are required to do anyway—by providing you a means of publishing the written work you must produce in order to graduate.

Law review members are generally required to write a note or comment during their first year on the journal in order to become an editor during their second year. Along with fulfilling the ABA writing requirement, many of these student pieces are published, although the number of published student notes and comments depends upon each particular law review's policies.

Obviously, there are tremendous benefits to having a published legal article. For one thing, it adds another valuable line to the "legal" section of your résumé. For another, it provides an interesting topic of conversation to bring up with potential employers. Indeed, employers often ask about a note or a comment a student may be working on even if it is not yet published. Lastly, not only does publication show that a given student has achieved an additional important milestone during law school, but also that the student has enough analytical ability and writing skills to put together a publishable legal article.

Note: In addition to appearing in print form, published law review articles (including student-written notes and comments) are permanently archived online through Westlaw and LexisNexis.

6. Potential Future Benefits—The Unknown Variable

Even if all of the incentives discussed above do not entice you to try and get onto your school's law review, you should keep in mind that, although you don't think you need it now, you may want the credential at some point in the future. Even if you do not currently think you will ever want to serve as a judicial law clerk, work at a top law firm, or be a law professor, your plans may change. Besides, adding law review membership to your résumé would have a positive impact on your chances for employment in almost *any* legal job. And remember, even if you don't plan on working as an attorney after law school, you never know when, at some point in the future, you might say to yourself: "I've got a law degree, why not be a lawyer?"

In many ways, this is the most powerful incentive to try and get on law review, because you never know when you might need to pull out your résumé and rely on the few lines of text printed thereon. And no matter where you end up applying to work in the future, it will never hurt you to have law review on your résumé, but it could potentially help you out immensely. I have never heard of someone being denied a job because she had law review on her resume, but thousands of students every year are overlooked by employers because they lacked the law review credential.

At this point, you might be thinking, "Yeah, sure, I know law review membership has tons of benefits. But being on law review can't be entirely pleasant and beneficial, can it?" No, it can't. Law students sometimes say that being on law review is like eating your vegetables—most students feel that they should do it even if they don't really want to. The reason some law students are wary of joining law review is that, while law review membership has many advantages, it also has the following drawbacks, which you should be aware of before jumping on the law review bandwagon:

Drawbacks

1. Time Consuming

Accepting membership on the law review is a major time commitment. It means agreeing to spend several hours per week on law review-related tasks for the rest of law school, usually including summers. This type of time commitment can be especially burdensome on law students because the time-squeeze placed on them by law classes and extracurricular activities (including family obligations) is usually already substantial. So, those students fortunate

Note: Law reviewers have been known to spend many late nights in a dark corner of the library poring over legal articles about obscure areas of the law.

enough to get onto the law review inevitably find themselves stretched very thin between their journal duties and their other academic and personal commitments.

One result of this is that law review members often must work during weekends and vacations. The incredible time demands of law review can put a further strain on relationships and on friendships, not to mention on your sanity (which may already be hanging by a thread due to the stress from your law school classes). As a result, being on law review can sometimes feel more like being stuck in a trap than being up on a pedestal.

The difficulty of balancing the time demands of law review membership with the heavy workload of law school classes can become almost overwhelming. Because of this, it is not uncommon for law review members' grades to slip a bit once assuming their journal duties. However, since the prestige of the law review credential equals, if not exceeds, that of *Order of the Coif* (top 10% GPA at graduation), it is not advisable to turn down law review membership solely to protect your GPA.

In addition, most students who manage to get on law review should be able to cope with the demands placed on them through their law review membership. Indeed, as noted before, employers will take your ability to juggle the demands of your classes and your law review commitments as a positive indicator of your future performance. Nonetheless, it is important to know about this potential drawback of law review membership before joining up.

2. Tedious

Not only is the work demanded by law review membership time-consuming, but much of it is also very detail-oriented and dull. In a word: tedious. This is particularly true with the duties delegated to the first-year members of the law review.

One duty often assigned to first-year members is cite-checking and micro-editing a specific portion of an article being considered for publication. This entails being sent around the library to get printed copies of every authority cited by the author to check first hand whether every citation is spot on, every quote exact, and every comma conforming to the citation style manual—at most law schools, the "Bluebook" (e.g., should the comma be italicized or not?). Although this mind-numbing exercise teaches you a little about correctly applying the Bluebook rules, you don't really learn much about the article you're cite checking because you've only been given a tiny fragment of it—you're not really "reading" it so much as examining it under a microscope to remove any minute flaws it may have.

On the other hand, first-year members also spend a significant amount of time writing their own legal article, which is itself a valuable experience. In addition, second year law review members' tasks are generally somewhat more "interesting," such as editing and revising entire legal articles (rather than micro-editing small chunks). So although the law review can appear to be tortuously tedious, there's a light at the end of the tunnel for those first-year law reviewers.

3. Obscure and Theoretical

The basis of every successful law review article is a novel legal argument. That is, it has to contain an argument that no one has ever made before on paper. As you can imagine, this principal leads to many law review articles being written on very narrow and obscure points of law. And while delving into such little-known areas of the law can be interesting (although, as you can imagine, it can also be torture), it generally does not add much value to your overall legal education.

Also, it is worth noting that since the law review is an academic journal, the articles published therein often analyze new or undecided areas of the law, focusing on their theoretical foundations rather than their practical applications. These theoretical arguments often serve only to "explore" a legal topic and have little to no impact in the real world.

That said, courts—including the U.S. Supreme Court—have relied on law review articles in order to decide cases. (For example, the Supreme Court in *John Hancock Mutual Life Insurance Company v. Harris Trust & Savings Bank*, 510 U.S. 86 (1993), quotes a student comment from the *Northwestern University Law Review* to support an assertion of law.) But, needless to say, chances are any article you, as a law review member, would edit or write will not serve as the linchpin authority responsible for a decision by the nation's highest court.

4. Law Review Backlash

Not everyone will be happy to see you make law review. Inevitably, some students in every class who are not on law review hold a grudge against law review members for a number of reasons, including sour grapes. This animosity toward law reviewers is evident at law schools owing to, for example, the comments made by these disgruntled students, such as, "Law review is a waste of time, I didn't even bother entering the competition," or, "Everyone on law review is a snob ... they all think they're better than everyone else." Such attitudes are present at most (if not all) law schools, and law review members must be prepared for the measurable unpopularity that accompanies law review membership.

Personally, I highly recommend students try to get on the law review or a specialty journal, if they can. Like in any endeavor, if one looks for reasons not to do it, one will find them.[2] But, in my opinion, the potential benefits for most students are simply too great to justify passing up the opportunity.

Chapter 3

Methods of Getting onto the Law Review

The path to law review membership varies slightly from law school to law school, but virtually always contains a combination of some or all of the following elements. Most law reviews select members after their first year of studies either through a writing competition (known as "writing-on" to the law review), their first-year grades (known as "grading-on" to the law review), or some combination thereof (known as "composite-on"). A number of schools will also grant membership to students who independently submit a publishable article (known as "noting-on"). The write-on competition usually requires applicants to compose a written analysis of a specific legal topic, often based on a recent Supreme Court decision or a circuit split. The written submissions are usually a set length and applicants are typically provided with a packet of "source materials," which serve as the exclusive authorities upon which each applicant can rely as support for his or her submission paper claim.

Generally, all of the methods of gaining law review membership, except grade-on, require students to write a competition paper in order to apply for membership. In addition to these methods, some specialized law journals offer a non-competitive avenue for gaining membership to them: "walk-on." Here is a brief overview of these basic methods of gaining law review membership:

Method #1: *Grade-On*

Some law reviews offer membership to the very top students in each first-year class. The number of students accepted through grade-on varies from law school to law school, but it is almost invariably a very low number. For example, the *Connecticut Law Review* accepts only six members as grade-ons out of the 24 members it accepts annually.[1] That means that only the top six students—not six percent, but six *students*—based on their first-year grades are invited onto the *Connecticut Law Review* each year.

Similarly, the *San Diego Law Review* extends grade-on invitations to the top five percent of its day division students each year,[2] the *Suffolk University Law Review* extends grade-on invitations to the three top-ranking students from each first-year section and the top student in the second-year evening division,[3] and the *University of Miami Law Review* extends invitations to the top ten percent of the first-year class.[4] A notable exception to this trend of offering very few grade-on membership invitations is the *University of Chicago Law Review*, which extends two-thirds of its membership invitations based solely on first-year grades (provided that the candidate participated in the write-on competition).[5]

As you can see, very few students grade-on to the law review. And, typically, first-year students do not receive their spring grades until after the write-on competition has taken place, meaning that even if you are at the top of your class after the first semester (and congratulations if you are!), you should still participate in the write-on competition just in case you slip out of the top spot. In addition, most law reviews require that even grade-on candidates participate in the write-on competition, meaning that even if you are at the top of the class, you will not receive an invitation based on your grades unless you submit a write-on paper.

Method #2: *Write-On*

For those law students not fortunate enough to finish their first-year at the top of their class grade-wise (i.e., the vast majority of students), the only way to get on law review is through success in the write-on competition. As mentioned before, the competition (discussed in detail in Chapter 4) usually requires candidates to write a short and persuasive legal article using a set of uniform source materials. Some law schools also require applicants to complete an editing exercise and/or submit a personal statement.

Many law reviews accept some or most new members exclusively through their performance in the write-on competition. Those law reviews that do so select the best papers from the competition and invite the authors of those papers to be members of the law review, regardless of their grades. Members selected in this manner are said to "write-on" to the law review.

A few law reviews accept *all* their new members as write-ons. For example, the *California Law Review* accepts new members based entirely on their performance in the write-on competition (consisting of a written casenote, an editing exercise, and a personal statement); they do not take grades into account whatsoever.[6] However, this is the exception rather than the rule. A more typical policy is that of the *New York University Law Review*, which selects about one-third of its members based solely on the write-on competition results.[7]

Method #3: *Composite-On*

Most law reviews accept several members through a combination of their performance in the write-on competition and first-year grades and/or another measure, such as an editing exercise or a personal statement. In fact, this is probably the most common way students gain journal membership. Students who get on law review in this manner are said to "composite-on."

The composite-on selection process is similar to the law school admissions procedure in that it involves combining two (or more) quantitative scores into a single composite number. But whereas the quantitative numbers combined in the admissions process consist of students' undergraduate GPA and LSAT scores, the composite-on process combines students' first-year grades with their scores on the write-on competition. And just like law school admissions, the candidates with the highest composite numbers (above a certain cut-off number) are invited to join the law review.

Law reviews differ greatly in how they calculate the composite number and in the number of memberships they offer through this method (as opposed to through grade-on or write-on). As mentioned above, the *California Law Review* does not extend a single membership based on a composite number, instead inviting only write-on candidates to join their journal. The *Harvard Law Review*, on the other hand, has a more typical membership selection policy. Forty-six students are invited to join the *Harvard Law Review* each year — twenty are selected based solely on their write-on competition scores, fourteen are selected based on a combination of grades and competition scores, and twelve are selected based on a holistic but anonymous review.[8]

Method #4: *Note-On*

Some law reviews offer one last shot at membership for those who did not make it onto the law review following the write-on competition. It's called "noting-on." In order to get on law review through this method, law students typically must write a full-length publishable student note and submit it to the law review editorial board. This note-on competition can take place anywhere from October of the Two-L year to November of the Three-L year. Law reviews that include a noting-on admissions process include the *California Law Review*,[9] the *Washington Law Review*,[10] and the *Illinois Law Review*,[11] though several law reviews do not extend any membership offers through a process of this kind.

Method #5: *Walk-On*

The final method of gaining journal membership is normally offered only as a way of becoming a member of a specialty law journal. This is the "walk-on" method, and it essentially amounts to showing up to the journal's office and signing up for membership.

It is highly unlikely that any law review offers membership in this manner. This is because law reviews usually have many more applicants than they have spaces available for new members. In truth, law reviews deny membership to the vast majority of those who apply. Specialty law journals, on the other hand, sometimes have openings available for interested students to sign up and participate in the journal, without putting them through any type of competitive process.

Chapter 4

An Overview of the Write-On Competition

With few exceptions, the only way to gain membership to the law review is to participate in the One-L write-on competition. Unfortunately for students, the competition usually takes place either during spring break of their first year or following the spring semester finals, meaning it is held at a time when most students are hoping to purge their minds of any thought of law school. The good news is that because it takes place at such an inconvenient time, some students choose not to participate or not to take it too seriously, giving those who are dedicated an added advantage.

Write-on competitions vary from law school to law school and from year to year. Nevertheless, there are some general guidelines (discussed in chapters 5 through 8) that should be adhered to regardless of the format of your school's competition. And the vast majority of competitions contain certain elements in common, which will be discussed below.

The Main Assignment

In a typical write-on competition, students are given a main assignment, which requires them to write a short persuasive essay (called a "submission paper") on an issue chosen by those organizing the competition. For example, the competition instructions might direct students to: "Express and defend your views on whether medical treatment can qualify an individual as 'disabled' under the Americans with Disabilities Act"; or "Analyze and critique the recent *Blakely v. Washington* case."

Along with the instruction page, students are normally given a prepared set of source materials. Most competitions are "closed universe," meaning students are not allowed to use any materials outside of those provided to them. Normally, the student's job is to choose which side of the issue to argue and to defend his or her argument as persuasively as possible, utilizing only the source materials provided.

On the other hand, some competitions provide students no particular issue to write about. If your competition turns out to be of this type, your job will include finding an interesting issue to write about which is discussed in the materials.

Students are given a time limit for finishing and submitting their paper, and are usually also given a page or word limit. The time limit can range from four days (e.g., the *George Washington University Law Review*'s write-on competition)[1] to two weeks (e.g., the *NYU Law Review*'s write-on competition).[2] The page limit is usually no more than 10 pages of text and 15 pages of endnotes. Law reviews tend to keep the permissible length of submission papers to a minimum because of the difficulty of grading dozens of submissions in a short period of time.

Students are also given detailed instructions on the required format and structure of the submission paper, including which font must be used, which margins must be applied, and even how the pages must be numbered. These instructions, along with any other instructions included with the competition materials, should be followed to a T.

Submission papers are normally graded blindly, being identified only by a number which the graders will not be able to associate with a particular student. Each paper is assigned a score based on a laundry list of criteria, such as legal analysis, persuasiveness, use of authorities, grammar, punctuation, and adherence to the competition instructions. In order to remove statistical variations in the grading scale, most law reviews ensure that every submission paper is evaluated by several graders.

Casenote vs. Comment

There are two primary types of articles that students are asked to draft in the write-on competition. There is no uniformity, however, with regard to what these two categories of articles are called among the various law reviews.

In *Scholarly Writing for Law Students*, Professors Elizabeth Fajans and Mary R. Falk give a comprehensive overview of the two types of student-written articles.[3] Here, I will provide a brief summary. The first type of article analyzes a single case. Some law reviews call this type of article a "casenote," while others call it a "case comment," "comment," or "note."[4] The other type of article analyzes a particular area of the law, and different law reviews usually call these articles either "comments" or "notes."[5]

For simplicity's sake, this book will refer to the one-case analyses as "casenotes," and to the articles analyzing an area of the law as "comments."[6]

Casenotes

The majority of law review competitions require students to write a casenote. The purpose of this type of article is to provide a thoughtful and original evaluation of the court's decision in a particular case—not to merely summarize it.

As articulated in *Scholarly Writing for Law Students*, "a successful casenote always looks beyond a court's articulated reasons for its decision and beyond the dissent's articulated reasons for disagreement. It is, therefore, never sufficient to argue that the majority is correct for the very reasons the majority advances, nor is it sufficient to argue that the majority is wrong for the very reasons advanced by the dissent."[7] A casenote must analyze the applicable law and come to an original conclusion about why the court got it right or got it wrong.

As categorized by Professors Fajans and Falk, the following are some examples of the types of analyses that a successful casenote can yield:

- The result was correct, but the court proposed no clear standard for guidance in future; XYZ would be a workable standard.

- The result was incorrect; the court creates an exception to a constitutional provision that could swallow the rule.

- The result was incorrect; the court failed to look to the larger social context.

- The result is incorrect; the court's interpretation is at odds with the goals of the statute.

- The result was correct; further, the court's standard is so complex that the outcome of future cases cannot be predicted; ABC would be a better standard.

- The result was correct, but the ruling protects one constitutional guarantee while endangering another.

- The result was correct, but the court's reasoning obscured the proper inquiry.

- The result was incorrect; the court failed to consider a significant issue which would have been dispositive.

- The result was correct; however, the decision appears to overrule sub silentio an important line of cases.

- The result was incorrect; it will result in an inefficient allocation of resources.

- The result was incorrect; the court misconstrued or misused precedent.[8]

A casenote should contain four parts: introduction, background, analysis, and conclusion.[9] "[T]he casenote follows a virtually unvarying four-part pattern: introduction, background, analysis, conclusion. The introduction describes the case and its holding very briefly and plainly states the writer's thesis: 'In this note (paper), I argue that....' It also provides a roadmap: 'Part I describes X; Part II analyzes Y.'"[10] The background should include a summary of the facts of the case, its procedural history, and the court's reasoning, as well as that of the concurring and dissenting opinions.[11]

The analysis section of the casenote occupies the vast majority of the paper, and contains the substance of the writer's claim — i.e., why the court got it right or wrong and, perhaps, what the correct outcome should be. The conclusion is a short summary of the analysis, and may also be used to address issues that are raised by the writer's claim.[12]

Comments

Occasionally, write-on competitions require students to draft a comment, which analyzes an area of the law, as opposed to focusing on a single case. But there are many distinct types of comments out there, and it is important that you have knowledge of each of them just in case you are asked to write a specific type of comment in the competition. Another reason you should be aware of the different comments out there is that you may choose to write a particular type of comment based on the argument you formulate.

One of the most comprehensive categorizations of comments was performed by Professor Richard Delgado, who identified ten distinct sub-categories of comments.[13] Here, in Professor Delgado's words, are the ten different types of comments:

[1] First, there is the "case cruncher" — the "typical" article. This type of article analyzes case law in an area that is confused, in conflict, or in transition. Doctrine is antiquated or incoherent and needs to be reshaped. Often the author resolves the conflict or problem by reference to policy, offering a solution that best advances goals of equity, efficiency, and so forth.

[2] Next, there is the law reform article. Pieces in this vein argue that a legal rule or institution is not just incoherent, but bad — has evil consequences, is inequitable or unfair. The writer shows how to change the rule to avoid these problems.

[3] There is also the legislative note, in which the author analyzes proposed or recently enacted legislation, often section by section, offering comments, criticisms, and sometimes suggestions for improvement.

[4] Another type of article is the interdisciplinary article. The author of an interdisciplinary article shows how insights from another field, such as psychology, economics, or sociology, can enable the law to deal better with some recurring problem....

[5] There is the theory-fitting article. The author examines developments in an area of law and finds in them the seeds of a new legal theory or tort....

[6] Discussions of the legal profession, legal language, legal argument, or legal education form yet another category of law review writing....

[7] There are the bookish, learned dialogues that continue a pre-existing debate. These pieces take the following form: "In an influential article in the W Law Review, Professor X argued Z. Critics, including Professor Y, attacked her view, arguing A, B, and C. This Article offers D, a new approach to the problem of Z (a new criticism, a new way of defending X's position in the face of her critics, a way of accommodating X and her critics, or something of the sort)."

[8] Another category consists of pieces on legal history. The origins and development of a legal rule or institution may shed light on its current operation or shortcomings.

[9] Similarly, comparative law articles are often valuable and engrossing for many of the same reasons: it will sometimes happen that other legal systems treat a problem more effectively or more humanely than does ours.[14]

The tenth, and final, type of comment identified by Professor Delgado is the empirical research article, which is "in some ways, the most useful of all, if one can manage the logistical problems it presents, because it enables the writer to expand knowledge beyond the armchair confines limiting most legal writing."[15]

Although this list is quite comprehensive, there may be yet other types of comments out there. But don't worry about memorizing this or any other list of comment types. It is sufficient to simply be aware that there are many different kinds of them out there. Of course, if your write-on competition asks you to write a specific type of comment, you must write precisely that type. As mentioned above—and will be repeated below—you must follow the competition instructions scrupulously.

Like casenotes, comments consist of four basic parts; an introduction, a background section, an analysis section, and a short conclusion. These sections are identical to those of a casenote, except that the comment deals with an area of the law rather than critiquing the outcome of a particular case.

Other Possible Tasks

In addition to the main assignment, some law reviews require students to do an editing assignment, which consists of a few pages of separate text containing dozens of intentionally planted errors. The student's job is to find the errors and correct them, using the particular editing symbols provided to you with the competition materials. Students are typically instructed to use the Bluebook or some other specific citation manual as a guide to making their edits. If so, the assigned manual should be followed down to the smallest detail (e.g., whether a particular comma should be italicized). The editing exercise is discussed in greater detail in Chapter 7.

Finally, the write-on competition may also require students to submit a personal statement. This topic will be discussed in greater detail in Chapter 8, so it is sufficient to say here that the personal statement should be interesting and as well-written as possible.

In a nutshell, the student's job in the write-on competition is to produce the best-written, best-bluebooked, and most persuasive submission paper possible; to proofread and bluebook the editing assignment thoroughly (if there is one); draft an interesting and well-written personal statement (if there is one); and, above all, to scrupulously follow all the instructions.

Chapter 5

Preparing for the Write-On Competition

In order to maximize your chances of succeeding in the write-on competition, it is essential to begin preparing several weeks before it starts. Of course, the competition comes at a time when you are most likely swamped with other work (either during spring break or after spring semester finals), so finding the time to prepare can be difficult. But it is absolutely necessary. If you go into the write-on competition unprepared, you will have virtually no chance of performing well enough to be selected for law review membership.

You should prepare for the write-on competition much the same way you probably prepared for the LSAT exam; by finding out as much as you can regarding what to expect in the competition and preparing yourself to perform to the best of your abilities. Specifically, there are five activities you should perform in order to maximize your chances of success in the competition: attend the law review informational meeting, clear your schedule, learn the Bluebook, read old competition papers, and set the right environment. Each of these activities will be discussed in detail below.

Preparation Activity 1: *Attend the Law Review Informational Meeting*

This first piece of preparation advice is so obvious that it shouldn't have to be said, but is so important that it couldn't be left out of this book: Do not miss the law review informational meeting at your school (if one is held). Almost all law review editorial boards put on an informational meeting during the spring semester, at least a couple of weeks before the write-on competition. At the meeting, the editors generally discuss the format of the competition and give some pointers regarding what they are looking for in submission papers. They sometimes even hand out a sample student note or comment, or a submission paper from a previous competition, to those in attendance as an exemplar of what the graders will be looking for.

Needless to say, the information given by the editors at this meeting is invaluable, and attending the meeting is an important first step in your preparation for the write-on competition. If, however, you are unable to attend the meeting, the editor-in-chief or another law review member may be available to discuss the law review and the write-on competition with those interested.

Preparation Activity 2: *Clear Your Schedule*

As soon as you find out the dates of the write-on competition, you should make sure that you have no other obligations during that period of time. This means no vacations, no working, and no performing other avoidable activities. If you find that you have a conflicting activity, try to cancel or reschedule it.

It is crucial that you clear your calendar because the write-on competition lasts only a short period of time (between three and fourteen days), and every hour of the competition is valuable. Between reading through the materials, outlining your argument, writing, and revising your paper, you will most likely need every minute of the time allotted.

But putting this time aside exclusively for the write-on competition takes some planning ahead, particularly in light of the fact that it takes place either during spring break or during the first week following the spring semester final exams. During spring break, friends and family may plan to take a vacation with you, and during the first couple of weeks of the One-L summer, it is very tempting to either just relax by taking a break from the law or to begin your summer job immediately. However, in order to maximize your chances of success in the competition, it is imperative that you put everything else aside during that week or two and concentrate only on the competition.

If your write-on competition takes place after your spring semester final exams, tell your summer employer that you want to begin work a week or two after the end of the school year. Likewise, if your family invites you to visit them during spring break, tell them you will arrive a few days later. Additionally, if you have young children, try and have the other parent or someone else spend more time with them during the week of the competition. Planning ahead in this way could prove to be one of the most valuable decisions you make in law school.

But if you can't get out of your other obligations, you should not use that as an excuse to skip the competition altogether. One law review member I spoke with while preparing to write this book told me that, although she was going to law school in Boston, she had to attend a wedding in Seattle during the write-on competition. What's worse, her mother booked her airplane ticket to return to Boston after the submission papers were due! So, she had to spend the last four days during the competition writing in a hotel room, and had to send her submission paper to Boston by way of express mail in order for it to arrive on time. Despite all of this, she made it onto law review.

As you can see from that student's story, even with significant interruptions during the competition (such as working, traveling, studying, or taking care of the children) it is still possible to write a successful submission paper and make it onto the law review. But it is undoubtedly easier to do so if you are able to eliminate such distractions and focus exclusively on the competition.

Preparation Activity 3: *Maximize Your Knowledge of the Bluebook*

A significant portion of your score in the write-on competition will be based on your bluebooking proficiency—i.e., your ability to cite the source materials using the correct style and format. Given the influence your knowledge of the Bluebook will have on your success in the competition, you should familiarize yourself with the Bluebook citation rules *prior* to the competition.

A good starting point for accomplishing this goal is to read the Bluebook from cover to cover, concentrating on the formatting differences between body text citations and footnote citations. Next, you should practice, practice, practice. Try citing cases from several different courts, federal and state statutes, the Constitution, treatises, law review articles, and books. All the while, you should familiarize yourself with where to find the rules regarding each type of citation in the Bluebook. You never know which type of authorities will show up in the competition and you should be prepared to cite anything they may throw at you.

You can also improve your bluebooking skills while writing for your classes by paying close attention to the particular style and format of specific citations. It is helpful, for example, to know commonly used citation formats by heart, such as that of law review articles: author, article name (in italics), volume number, journal abbreviation (in small caps), first page, specific page(s), and year.[1]

Another helpful tip is to tab your Bluebook. Not only will this save you from wasting time flipping through the index during the competition, but it will help you memorize where certain rules are as you go through inserting tabs.

Note: Some law schools may use a citation manual other than the Bluebook, such as the *ALWD Citation Manual* or the *California Style Manual.* You should familiarize yourself with whichever citation manual your law school follows.

Pay particularly close attention to the section of the Bluebook listing the words that must be abbreviated in case names (found in Table T.6). It's easy to forget to abbreviate many of those words, and failing to do so would result in a lower score for your write-on submission paper. But keep in mind that case names written in the body text of your paper should not be abbreviated in the same way as those listed in footnotes. Another section to pay close attention to is the one on signals, such as *"see also," "accord,"* and *"cf."* These will be very important to be familiar with while writing your competition paper.

Other Common Bluebooking Errors

The following are some of the most common bluebooking mistakes students make in the write-on competition. It pays, therefore, to pay close attention to the sections in the Bluebook addressing these topics.

Of course, you could choose to simply wait until the competition rolls around and look up every specific citation style and format as you write your paper, but this would waste a lot of your precious time during the competition. The amount of time you will save through greater familiarity with the Bluebook will more than compensate for the time you spend before the competition familiarizing yourself with it.

Topic	Error	Bluebook Rule
Signals	Failure to use or incorrect use of introductory signals	Rules 1.2 & 1.3
Order	Failure to put intrajurisdictional cites of the same court level in reverse chronological order	Rule 1.4
	Failure to alphabetize state cites	Rule 1.4
Parentheticals	Failure to include parenthetical information when necessary	Rule 1.5
	Failure to use present participle to begin parenthetical	Rule 1.5
	Capitalization error	Rule 1.5

Topic	Error	Bluebook Rule
Statutes	Failure to cite current statute	Rule 12.3
	Failure to cite session laws when appropriate	Rule 12.4
Case Names	Incorrect abbreviation and incorrect use of geographical terms	Rule 10.2.1(f)
Courts	Failure to use correct abbreviations	Rule 10.4
Reporters	Failure to abbreviate and space correctly	Rules 10.1-10.2
	Failure to include parallel citations	Rule 10.3.1
	Incorrect reporter for the court	Rule 10.3.2
Articles	Failure to use correct typeface	Rule 16
	Failure to abbreviate law reviews correctly	Table T.14
	Failure to properly indicate volume number and date of review and page number of article	Rule 16
Miscellaneous	Incorrect typeface use in citation	Rule 2.1
	Failure to pinpoint page numbers	Rule 3.2(a)

Topic	Error	Bluebook Rule
Miscellaneous (continued)	Failure to use short citation form when necessary	Rules 4 & 10.9
	Incorrect use of "*Id.*," "*supra*," and "*hereinafter*"	Rules 4.1 & 4.2
	Failure to use block quotation when necessary	Rule 5.1
	Failure to use or incorrect use of brackets or ellipsis to indicate alteration of quote	Rules 5.2-5.3
	Incorrect capitalization or failure to capitalize when required	Rule 8

Bluebooking Quiz

If you have a few extra minutes, you might want to take a quick break from reading to play the bluebooking game. I'll admit, this might not be the most entertaining game in the world, but it is representative of what you might come across in the write-on competition.

To play, go through the following ten footnotes and see if you can find the citation errors (under the Bluebook rules). Some should be easy to spot but others are not. Use the Bluebook for assistance if necessary—you'll almost certainly be able to reference it in the competition. But remember that the more errors you can correct without assistance, the more time you will save in the actual competition. The answer key is in the Appendix on page 101.

Here we go!

[1] *Vanesa Ramirez vs. Sarah Boudreaux*, 322 F. 2d 25 (3rd Cir. 1996).

[2] 29 U.S.C. 1902-1911 (2007).

[3] *Jose Tolosa v. U.S.*, F.Supp.2d 88 (S.D. Cal. 2005).

⁴ *See also United Colonies Publishing v. City of Spokane*, 153 F.3d 441 (CA1 2006).

⁵ Natalia Salgado, <u>Immigration Inconsistencies: The Circuit Split on Fiancée Visas</u>, 115 Harv.L.Rev. 88, 95 (2002).

⁶ *Wade Construction, Inc. v. West Wynn Mfg. of Ireland*, 82 F.Supp. 233 (D.P.R. 1982).

⁷ *See* Robert Evans, *Property Acquisitions in Mineral Exploration*, 37 Rocky Mtn.Min.L.Inst. 581, 599 (1983).

⁸ *Hugo v. Thomas*, 221 Cal. Reporter 2d. 393 (Cal. Ct. App. 1993).

⁹ H.R. Rep. No. 88-702, at 43 (1954), *available at* 2 NLRB, Legislative History of the Internal Revenue Act, 1954, at 162 (1955).

¹⁰ <u>Convention for the Agreement on Free Trade</u>, Aug. 22, 2004, United States-Argentina, 46 U.S.T. 1184.

If some of the errors thrown into these footnotes seem to be sneaky and/or downright dirty, that's because they are. Sorry about that. But these nitpicky and anal-retentive mistakes are just the type you will find in the actual bluebooking exercise (if your school has one) in the write-on competition. Moreover, these are the types of errors that editors will pick up on and mark you down for if they are found in your submission paper.

> *Note:* In addition to the Bluebook, it is a very good idea to read through a style guide in order to brush up on your writing technique before the competition. One great option on this front is Strunk & White's "The Elements of Style." And if you are allowed to use a style guide while writing your competition paper, by all means, use it!

So you are well-advised to review the Bluebook—or any other citation manual your law school subscribes to—until you are able to pick up on most, if not all, of these types of citation errors. Of course, you don't need to be able to correct them from memory since you'll be permitted to use the Bluebook during the competition. But you should at least be able to identify the spots where there are or may be errors.

Preparation Activity 4: *Read Old Submission Papers and Published Student Casenotes and Comments*

While preparing for the write-on competition, you should get your hands on all available information pertaining to your school's competition. This includes competition rules and guidelines, past competition instructions, and old submission papers by students who made it onto law review.

Some law reviews make prior years' submission papers available for students to review. If so, you should pay close attention to the format, writing style, and argument of that submission paper, since it was chosen as a representative example for a reason. Also, if you are able to get your hands on other successful submission papers (e.g., from current and past law review members from your school), those can also be a valuable resource in your preparation for the competition.

It is also a good idea to read one or more student notes or comments published by your school's law review. Those published student pieces went through months of rigorous editing by multiple editors and should be polished to the point of near perfection (at least technically). You can learn a lot about what is expected from a high quality write-on submission by reading a published student note or comment, although no one expects a submission paper to match the written quality of a published piece.

Casenote Excerpt

As a starting point, you may want to review the casenote excerpt below, which was published in the *Washington Law Review*.[2] It contains citations to statutes, regulations, a website, a treatise, and cases from the federal courts of appeal and from immigration courts. Because it contains citations to a broad cross section of authorities, it should serve as a helpful introduction and/or review of the citation format required by the Bluebook for footnotes and endnotes. This is especially true in light of the citations to immigration courts, which underscore the need to memorize citations to unfamiliar sources such as specialized tribunals.

This excerpt should also give you a sense of what the editors will be looking for in the competition papers. Keep in mind, however, that your competition's instructions may require you to write in a slightly different style than what is presented here. For example, some law reviews require students to limit their endnotes to only a few lines of text. Thus, some of the footnotes in the excerpt below would be too long for those competitions.

Remember, always follow the competition instructions. The following excerpt is intended only as a generic example of what is normally required of students in the write-on competition.

* * *

I. A NONCITIZEN MAY BE GRANTED ASYLUM IF HE OR SHE QUALIFIES AS A REFUGEE UNDER THE INA

To qualify for asylum, a noncitizen applicant has the burden of establishing that he or she is a refugee as defined in § 101(a)(42)(A) of the Immigration and Nationality Act (INA).[1] This section defines a refugee as a person who is outside of his or her country of nationality and is unable or unwilling to return to that country because of a well-founded fear of persecution on account of race, religion, nationality, membership in a particular social group, or political opinion.[2] The "persecution" element imposes a high standard that the applicant must meet, and requires more than a showing of

---

1. 8 U.S.C. § 1101(a)(42)(A) (2000). The U.S. Attorney General, normally represented by asylum officers, may grant asylum to any applicant who qualifies as a refugee and is not barred by any of the grounds for inadmissibility. *Id.* § 1158(b)(1)-(2). Unsuccessful applicants can appeal the asylum officer's decision to an immigration court, 8 C.F.R. § 208.31(g) (2004); then to the BIA, *id.* § 1003.1(b); and then to the United States Court of Appeals in the circuit where the original application was filed. *See* United States Department of Justice, Executive Office for Immigration Review, Board of Immigration Appeals, P 3, at http:// www.usdoj.gov/eoir/biainfo .htm (last visited Mar. 21, 2005) ("All Board decisions are subject to judicial review in the Federal courts."). Throughout this process, the applicant bears the burden of establishing asylum eligibility under INA § 101(a)(42)(A). 8 C.F.R. § 208.13(a).

2. 8 U.S.C. § 1101(a)(42)(A).

offensive treatment.[3] In addition, the applicant must show that his or her fear of persecution is "well-founded."[4] An applicant may show a well-founded fear of persecution by demonstrating that there is a reasonable possibility that the applicant would suffer persecution upon returning to the applicant's home country.[5]

A. To Be Eligible for Asylum, an Applicant Must Show Harm that Rises to the Level of Persecution

To demonstrate persecution under INA § 101(a)(42)(A), an applicant must show extreme harm[6] that either occurred in the past or may occur in the future.[7] This extremity requirement does not limit persecution to severe physical harm[8] or threats to life or freedom,[9] such as severe beatings,[10] torture,[11] or fear of death.[12] Rather, courts have held

---

3. Fatin v. INS, 12 F.3d 1233, 1243 (3d Cir. 1993).

4. 8 U.S.C. § 1101(a)(42)(A).

5. 8 C.F.R. § 208.13(b)(2)(i)(B).

6. *See Fatin*, 12 F.3d at 1243 ("'[P]ersecution' is an extreme concept that does not include every sort of treatment our society regards as offensive."); Kovac v. INS, 407 F.2d 102, 107 (9th Cir. 1969) ("'[P]ersecution' is too strong a word to be satisfied by proof of the likelihood of minor disadvantage or trivial inconvenience.").

7. *See* INA § 101(a)(42)(A) (codified at 8 U.S.C. § 1101(a)(42)(A)).

8. *See* Zhao v. Gonzalez, 2005 WL 590829, at *8 (5th Cir. Mar. 15, 2005) ("The harm or suffering need not be physical, but may take other forms...."); *accord In re* Laipenieks, 18 I. & N. Dec. 433, 456-57 (B.I.A. 1983) ("The harm or suffering need not [only] be physical...."), *rev'd on other grounds*, 750 F.2d 1427 (9th Cir. 1985).

9. *See* Cardoza-Fonseca v. INS, 767 F.2d 1448, 1452 (9th Cir. 1985) ("[T]he statutory term 'persecution' includes more than just restrictions on life and liberty....").

10. *See, e.g.*, Vladimirova v. Ashcroft, 377 F.3d 690, 696 (7th Cir. 2004) ("The physical violence suffered by petitioner—a beating so severe that it caused a miscarriage—certainly ... qualifies as proof of past persecution.").

11. *See, e.g., In re* S—P—, 21 I. & N. Dec. 486, 495-96 (B.I.A. 1996) (finding persecution in case of detention, interrogation, and torture); *In re* Acosta, 19 I. & N. Dec. 211, 222 n.9 (B.I.A. 1985) (discussing meaning of persecution; noting that "[t]he harm or suffering inflicted could consist of confinement or torture"), *overruled in part by In re* Mogharrabi, 19 I. & N. Dec. 439, 441 (B.I.A. 1987).

12. *See, e.g.*, Sotelo-Aquije v. Slattery, 17 F.3d 33, 35 (2d Cir. 1994) (holding that death threats by Shining Path guerrillas in Peru constituted persecution).

that persecution also includes lesser forms of physical harm.[13] In addition, courts may consider mental harm as an element—but not as the exclusive basis—of an applicant's persecution.[14]

Courts have held that female genital mutilation is extreme physical harm and that the future threat of it constitutes persecution of the applicant.[15] In *In re Kasinga*,[16] the Board of Immigration Appeals (BIA) granted asylum to a nineteen-year-old applicant who feared that she would be forced to undergo genital mutilation if removed to her home country of Togo.[17] In determining that the fear of female genital mutilation qualifies as persecution, the BIA reasoned that a "subjective 'punitive' or 'malignant' intent is not required for harm to constitute persecution."[18] No court has abrogated the BIA's holding in *Kasinga*; the few courts of appeals that have considered the same question have favorably cited the *Kasinga* board's holding.[19]

* * *

Again, keep in mind that the preceding excerpt should only be treated as a starting point. You must still review student-written articles in your school's law review and/or old submission papers in order

---

13. *See, e.g.*, Balazoski v. INS, 932 F.2d 638, 642 (7th Cir. 1991) (holding that "non-life-threatening violence and physical abuse" may constitute persecution).

14. *See* Shoaira v. Ashcroft, 377 F.3d 837, 844 (8th Cir. 2004) (concluding that "mental or emotional injury may in part constitute persecution"); Deborah E. Anker, *Law of Asylum in the United States* 215 (3d ed. 1999) (stating that mental harm can be "main element" of finding of persecution for asylum purposes).

15. *See* Mohammed v. Gonzales, No. 03-70803, slip op. 3063, 3068 n.2 (9th Cir. Mar. 10, 2005); Toure v. Ashcroft, No. 03-1706, 2005 WL 247942, at *6 n.4 (1st Cir. Feb. 3, 2005); *In re* Kasinga, 21 I. & N. Dec. 357, 368 (B.I.A. 1996).

16. 21 I. & N. Dec. 357 (B.I.A. 1996).

17. *Id.* at 358.

18. *Id.* at 365.

19. *See* Balogun v. Ashcroft, 374 F.3d 492, 499 (7th Cir. 2004); Azanor v. Ashcroft, 364 F.3d 1013, 1018-19 (9th Cir. 2004); Nwaokolo v. INS, 314 F.3d 303, 309 (7th Cir. 2002).

to get a clear picture of what is expected of students in your school's competition.

Whether you are reviewing old submission papers or published notes and comments, you should pay close attention to how the writings look aesthetically. The appearance, flow, and overall feel of your write-on submission will make a strong impression on those grading your paper and you want to make sure you do not hurt your chances of getting on law review by submitting a sloppy paper. (Aesthetics will be discussed more fully in Chapter 6, Subchapter 10.)

Preparation Activity 5: *Read the Papers You Wrote for Your First Year Legal Writing Course*

In your first year legal writing course, you will learn all of the fundamentals of how to draft legal documents. And your learning will take place, in large part, through practice. By the end of the year, you should have accumulated at least three or four papers that reflect the legal writing rules that you learned during the first year.

You should carefully read through each paper you wrote and make sure that you are still familiar with the rule you learned on that particular assignment — e.g., IRAC (issue, rule, analysis, conclusion). But don't just read the final version. Rather, you should read the first draft of each paper as well as the final copy, paying close attention to the mistakes you made the first time around. Doing this will make you much more familiar with the errors you tend to make, so you can watch out for them while writing your competition paper.

Preparation Activity 6: *Create an Appropriate Atmosphere*

During the write-on competition, you will spend several days buried in the materials and maxing out your brain power to produce the most brilliant legal argument possible in that short period of time. Considering the sacrifice you are making to participate in the competition, it is important that you give yourself every opportunity to succeed. This includes setting up an environment free from unnecessary distractions, allowing you to concentrate on writing your paper.

Of course, the most important component of setting the right environment was addressed under the Second Preparation Activity, above, i.e., clearing your schedule. But it is also important that you choose wisely *where* to write your submission paper.

Several law review members I spoke with told me that they wrote their submission papers in their law library, while others said they did it at home. One interviewee told me that she wrote her entire submission paper in a Starbucks coffee shop!

As for me, I chose to write my submission paper in my law school's library. I spent about eight or nine hours per day writing my competition paper, while I spent my evenings relaxing with my wife and hanging out with friends. That was the routine that worked for me.

But as you can see from the examples above, you must find a writing location and a routine that work for *you*. Some students loathe spending hours on end in the library while others cannot concentrate while studying at home. Whatever environment you found that worked for studying for final exams during your first-year of law school should also work well for writing your submission paper.

Chapter 6

Writing Your Submission Paper

The day has arrived to pick up the write-on competition packet and begin drafting your brilliant submission paper. But not so fast! The competition should be viewed as more of a marathon than a sprint. Pace yourself. The first thing you must do after picking up the competition packet is to take a deep breath, relax, and remind yourself: "I'm going to give this my best shot. No matter what happens, at least I know that I did everything in my power to succeed."

Now it's time to get to work.

Below is a timeline of the recommended approach to writing your submission paper. (The editing exercise and personal statement will be addressed in chapters 7 and 8, respectively.) I compiled this timeline based largely on my own experiences participating in the write-on competition and grading competition papers, but it also includes helpful advice from the dozens of current and former law review members whom I interviewed in preparation for writing this book.

Here's a quick summary of the timeline:

Step 1: Read and Re-Read the Instructions

Step 2: Read All the Source Materials

Step 3: Select a Claim

Step 4: Write a First Draft

Step 5: Do the Editing Exercise / Draft Your Personal Statement

Step 6: Revise and Organize Your Paper

Step 7: Proofread

Step 8: Maximize Your Paper's Aesthetic Quality

Step 9: Do a Final Proofread Before Submitting Your Paper

Each of the above-mentioned steps is discussed in detail below. You should read through the following material carefully, but keep in mind that your particular write-on competition may have requirements at odds with these suggestions. As mentioned earlier, *always* defer to your own competition's instructions.

Step 1: *Read and Re-Read the Instructions*

The single most important page in the entire competition packet is the instruction page. It will tell you exactly what the competition graders are looking for. As one law review member I spoke with put it, "Those students who scrupulously follow the instructions are the only ones who even have a shot at succeeding in the write-on competition."

Read through the instructions slowly and carefully, and make sure you understand each item. As you do so, keep in mind that the instructions are strict *rules*; not *guidelines*. Once you've read them once, read them once more.

In addition, you should re-read the instructions daily throughout the competition so as not to deviate from them at any point. They are usually very comprehensive and it is easy to overlook or forget one or two specific items as you get further along in the competition. But if you read them every day, they will stay fresh in your mind and you will be much more likely to follow them precisely.

At a minimum, the instructions typically cover:

a. How to *structure* the paper, such as which type of legal paper to write, how to break up the sections, and how long the paper may be;

b. How to *format* the paper, including which margins to use, how to organize the endnotes, and which font to use;

c. Which manual of *citations* to use (most likely the Bluebook);

d. Which *authorities* you may use in your research (the competitions are usually closed-universe); and

    e.   When and *how to submit* your paper.

The instructions may also include a description of the legal issues to be addressed in the paper. For example, one of the cases contained in the packet may address two very different legal issues: First Amendment freedom of speech and personal jurisdiction. If the instructions tell you to make a civil procedure argument using the materials, you know that the First Amendment part of the case will not be of use to you in writing your paper.

Keep in mind that the instructions are not suggestions; they must be meticulously followed. A group of hard working law review members spent a lot of time writing the instructions down and the law review graders severely penalize submission papers that do not conform to the instructions.

The purpose of requiring strict adherence to the competition rules is two-fold. First, rejecting papers for technical reasons makes grading much easier. Second, if you are selected to join law review, you will be expected to scrupulously follow the instructions of the senior members. Thus, if they ask you to italicize the first comma but not the second in "*see, e.g.,*" you'd better make sure that that second comma is never italicized.

The instructions may also include a suggested timeline for completing the assignment(s). Those same hardworking people who brought you the instructions should also be given deference in regard to the timeline, if any, that they suggest to you. If they made the effort to think up a timeline, it probably represents a useful way to split up your time in the competition. Do not hesitate to use their knowledge and experience to your advantage.

Important: Focus on the Prompt

Apart from providing comprehensive guidelines on how you must write your competition paper, the instructions also generally provide a statement of how you must frame your argument. The prompt may go something like this:

```
Using  only  the  materials  provided  in  this
packet,  write  a  legal  memorandum  articulating
```

```
whether a parent of an asylee may be granted
derivative asylum under INA §101(a)(42)(A),
based on the parent-child relationship.
```

Just remember, though the assignment may sound like the most uninteresting piece of nonsense you've ever had to write about, such obscure legal issues are what the law review is all about. And you have to play their game in order to join their club.

The prompt will provide you with the mental framework within which you should analyze the source materials provided in the rest of the packet (usually consisting of cases, statutes, and other legal materials). Thus, you should read the prompt a couple of times and keep it handy so you can refer back to it as you read through the rest of the materials. That way, you can constantly question how each authority is relevant to the issue in the prompt.

Step 2: *Read All the Source Materials*

Now that you have a good idea of what you are expected to write (from reading the instructions and the prompt), it is time to dig into the source materials provided in the competition packet. These materials may contain cases, statutes, excerpts from legal articles or treatises, or any other authorities that could possibly be used as support for a substantive legal argument.

There is no magical shortcut for how to get through the (most likely thick) stack of documents you must digest in order to choose and defend your legal claim. You've just got to *read the materials*. Moreover, it is important that you read *all* the materials *before* beginning to write.

Although each student has his or her own preferred method of how to approach lengthy research assignments (like the write-on competition), everyone should take notes while reading through the source materials, regardless of his or her own study habit idiosyncrasies. (For example, some students use tabs and margin-notes and others prefer to map out their argument on a separate page or computer file, but others prefer to read all the materials first before writing anything down. The first two above-mentioned methods may work on the write-on competition, but the latter one would be a bad idea.)

The time pressures and the stress from the competition may make it harder for you to remember important details than you may otherwise be accustomed to. Thus, regardless of your own particular study technique, it is highly recommended that you write your thoughts down as you read through the materials—whether it be

Note: Some write-on source materials contain a lengthy series of statutes, many of which may have nothing to do with the issue you are required to write about. Reading through pages and pages of irrelevant statutes would be a waste of your valuable time. Thus, you should read the title of each statute to determine which may be relevant, and focus on those. The other authorities in the source materials (such as cases) should also point you to the relevant statutes.

on the pages you're reading or on a separate page or computer file.

Keep in mind as you read through the source materials that your only goal in the competition is to formulate a persuasive and succinct argument on the issue presented in the prompt. As such, you should constantly question the relevance of each source to the issue in the prompt. The following questions are helpful to repeat to yourself as you read through the source materials:

- What factual similarities are there between the source and your particular problem?
- How can the source be utilized to support an argument on one side of the issue?
- How can the source be used in conjunction with other sources to bolster an argument for one side?

In addition, one law review member I spoke with pointed out that, as you read through the source materials, "You should keep an eye out for quotable passages that have particular relevance to the issue, since these can be particularly helpful in supporting the claim you end up choosing."

Moreover, do not pigeonhole yourself into searching for authorities that support one particular argument. For one thing, you should not make up your mind which side of the issue to argue on until you have read through all of the materials. For another, in order to formulate an effective legal argument, you must be familiar with all of the authorities on *both* sides of the issue in order to adequately address all possible counterarguments.

Finally, it is also important to avoid straying off onto tangential legal issues as this will cause you to lose valuable time and will add nothing to your final submission paper. However, be careful not to skip over a section of a source just because it appears irrelevant at first glance. Instead, read through each section of each source carefully to determine whether it is relevant to the issue in the prompt.

> *Note:* One of the best ways to give your submission paper an added advantage is to cite to authorities that support your claim in a creative way and may therefore be overlooked by other students making a similar claim. Accordingly, read through seemingly irrelevant sources carefully to see if there is an innovative way to use the source to support your argument.

Step 3: *Select a Claim*

Once you've read through all of the source materials, you need to choose which side of the issue to argue on. Typically, the prompt will require you come up with your own solution to the problem, but it may be written as either a command or a question. For example, the prompt could state:

```
Write a legal memorandum articulating whether
a parent of an asylee may be granted deriva-
tive asylum under INA §101(a)(42)(A).
```

Or the prompt could ask:

```
Can a parent of an asylee be granted deriva-
tive asylum based on his or her relationship to
the child?
```

Your job, then, is to come up with a legally supportable claim addressing the issue.

When the prompt is written as a question, your job would be to answer 'yes,' 'no,' or 'it depends,' and provide the underlying legal justification for your claim. For example: "Yes, because INA § 101(a)(42)(A) provides that a parent's suffering on account of her separation from her asylee child in the United States may provide the underlying justification for her own asylum claim."

Remember, most competitions are closed-universe, meaning that regardless of which argument might have more legal support in the real world, the only sources that matter for your purposes are those contained in the competition packet. So, if you've done prior research on the particular issue that serves as the subject of your competition paper, you should erase your prior knowledge of the subject during the competition and focus solely on the materials provided.

More often than not, the source materials will contain enough legal support for two (or more) sides of the issue to enable students to make an effective legal argument on either (or any) side. It normally doesn't matter which side you choose to argue on, as long as you can adequately support your claim with the authorities contained in the source materials. Nevertheless, there *are* a few pointers to keep in mind as you decide which claim to make:

a. Best Supported

You should choose the claim that you are best able to support with the authorities in the source materials. So, if the authorities clearly support a particular side of the issue, then that is the claim you should make. Also, as you analyze which side has the most supportive authority, take into account possible counterarguments. This will help you both focus on each claim's weaknesses and address the counterarguments to the claim you end up choosing.

b. Most Original

If the authorities in the source materials support more than one side of the argument equally, you should make the more creative argument, if there is one. Your number one priority in the write-on competition is to write a persuasive paper with a well-supported legal claim. If you can accomplish that goal while making a more original argument than most of your classmates, then you will likely earn a few extra points.

But be careful here. As one law review member told me, "Students should not get too cute in formulating their submission paper's argument. If they push the envelope outside what would normally be considered a solid legal claim, they will obviously be penalized for that."

c. Politically Correct

If the problem contains a politically-charged issue, try and avoid taking an unpopular stance in your paper. As a student you should be able to get a good idea of the political and ideological leanings of the general student population at your law school. Use that information to your advantage in the write-on competition by avoiding making an argument that you know the majority of the graders will disagree with.

d. All Else Being Equal, Flip a Coin

Sometimes neither side of the argument seems like a clear winner to you (i.e., neither side has more authoritative support, is more original, or is more politically safe). If that's the case, you should just flip a coin and go with one side. In the end, it does not matter which side you choose as long as you use the sources effectively and create a persuasive legal argument.

But be careful of the "it depends" argument. Take a close look at the prompt to be sure such a neutral argument is allowed before going forward with this type of claim.

> *Note:* You should re-read the prompt at this point to make sure that your claim speaks directly to the question posed in the problem. It is highly recommended that you re-read the prompt from time to time in addition to reviewing the instructions daily during the competition.

Step 4: *Write a First Draft*

Once you have read all the source materials and chosen a claim, you should write a rough draft of your paper. Although it may seem counter-intuitive, you should finish this first draft relatively quickly, and you need not pay too much attention to detail. Instead, what you want to accomplish at this stage is to get the basic framework of your claim down on paper (including citation to all major supporting authorities) so that it can be revised and edited into a polished argument later on.

Here are several important suggestions to keep in mind as you write your rough draft:

a. Follow the Instructions Regarding Structure and Format

As you write your rough draft, make sure that your structure and format comply with the instructions. It is much easier to make structural and formatting changes early in the writing process than it is to make them later on (when such changes can become a major overhaul rather than a minor detail). Having to adjust the margins after writing a full-length draft, for example, may usurp valuable time that would be better spent polishing your argument or refining your citations.

b. Make Effective Use of the Authorities

One of the criteria upon which your submission paper will be graded is how well you utilize the source materials to advance your argument. In order to maximize your score in this area, you should include a citation for each assertion you make which is supported by the authorities in the materials, and strive to cite to every one of the source materials at least once.

i. Make sure that seemingly inapplicable authorities are not somehow useful to your argument

Though there may be some authorities in the source materials that are truly not relevant to your argument, these, if there are any, will be few and far between. You should strive to cite to every authority even remotely helpful to your argument, whether as direct support for your claim or as a counterargument that must be addressed.

As mentioned above, just because an authority seems irrelevant at first glance does not mean it is truly inapplicable. Read through each authority carefully so as not to pass over potentially important sources.

ii. Differentiate between binding and persuasive authority

Unlike people, not all authorities are created equal. There will likely be a few principal sources (such as, for example, key Supreme Court cases or statutes) that constitute binding authority that you must follow. These authorities must either be cited as supporting authority for your argument or distinguished in some way.

The source materials will also likely include persuasive (i.e., non-binding) authorities, which must also be addressed in your paper. Some of these persuasive authorities may be helpful to your argument even if they don't appear to be so on first blush. But those papers which contain citations to less obvious, but nonetheless supportive, authorities will earn those hard-to-get points which can be the difference between a great submission paper and a mediocre one.

Note: Make sure to use non-binding authority only for its persuasive value, and not try and pass it off as mandatory. For example, if your entire claim is based on the "authority" of a law review article or a case from a different jurisdiction, you should rethink your argument. Try and base your claim on binding precedent or highly persuasive authority, and explain your reasons for doing so.

Although we all learn the difference between binding and persuasive authority during the first year of law school, the pressures of the write-on competition can make students overlook this important distinction and it is therefore a good idea to go into the competition with this distinction fresh in your mind.

Of the dozens of submission papers I read as a competition grader, most of them contained citations to all of the sources necessary to adequately support the legal claim they were making. But there were a few submission papers missing one or two such sources. Those authority-deficient papers received much lower scores in the "usage of authorities" grading category, and faced an uphill battle of trying to make the law review cut.

c. Add Footnotes or Endnotes as You Write, and Use All the Space Allowed for Citations

Although inserting footnotes or endnotes breaks the flow of writing to some extent, it takes much less time to do so as you draft your paper than to go back and do it after you've finished writing. If you wait until finishing your draft to add your citations, you may find yourself struggling to locate—or even remember—which authorities support a given passage. Thus, adding the footnotes or endnotes as you write will save you time. In addition, it will also help you gage the amount of space the footnotes or endnotes will take up.

Also, make sure you use all the space allowed for the citations, whether it is a specific number of footnotes or a specific number of pages of endnotes. Filling up the space allowed for citations will help you in a couple of ways. First, it will force you to include citations for all—or at least most—of your supportable assertions. And second, it will help your citation section conform aesthetically to what the graders are looking for. (See Subchapter 10 of this chapter, below, on aesthetics.)

d. Keep Paragraphs Generally Short and Vary the Sentence Length

As mentioned earlier, it is crucial that you make reading and understanding your submission paper as easy as possible for the graders. The easier it is for them to grasp your legal argument, the higher score you will get in the competition. One way to make your paper more readable to the graders is to keep your paragraphs short. Each paragraph should typically contain no more than four or five sentences. If a paragraph contains more than five sentences, re-read it and see if there is any way to say the same thing using fewer words.

Sometimes, however, you might find a paragraph absolutely must be longer than five sentences, particularly where some of those sentences are quite short. Don't sweat it. What is most important is to keep the average length of the paragraphs down to bite-size chunks that won't choke the reader. One way to ensure this happens is to ensure that your paragraphs' *average* word count is no more than 150 words. This can be checked easily in word processing programs such as Microsoft Word or WordPerfect.

Also, varying the sentence length tends to shake up the monotonous tone found in far too many submission papers. If you must write an extra-long sentence (which you should do only if absolutely necessary), try and follow it up with a short one. This will help keep the reader awake as he or she reads through your analysis, thereby improving your competition score.

e. Include Headings

Another way to make your paper more readable is to include headings, which give the graders a preview of each section of the paper, and also serve to supplement your argument. The importance of including headings is captured in this statement from a law reviewer I spoke with: "A submission paper without any headings is a headache to read and reflects poor writing. I graded three papers without headings, and I gave each one the low score it deserved." Ouch.

To maximize the effectiveness of your headings, make sure each one furthers your argument rather than simply states the issue addressed in that section. For example, instead of merely writing:

    IV. The Derivative Asylum Standard

it would be much more effective to write:

    IV. John Doe Satisfies the Derivative Asylum Standard Because He Is the Parent of an Asylee

If written most effectively, your headings should contain your entire argument (i.e., each point of the argument), as if it were written in a bullet-point format. As such, the graders should be able to understand the basic outline of your entire argument just by reading the headings. In addition, it may be appropriate to include subheadings if any single section of your paper spans more than a page-and-a-half or so.

f. Use Active Voice

There are several reasons you should avoid using the passive voice in your submission paper, but two of the most important ones are *readability* and *length*. Compare the following examples of passive and active voice:

Passive voice:

```
John Doe was stopped by Officer Smith on June
22, 2007.
```

Active voice:

```
Officer Smith stopped John Doe on June 22, 2007.
```

Both sentences convey the exact same information, but the one written in the passive voice is more difficult to read (because it is more awkward) and takes up more space. Nevertheless, many law students write in the passive voice in the write-on competition, much to their detriment. Legal writing should be clear, accurate, and brief, and the write-on competition is no exception.

One law review member told me, "We instruct our graders to deduct a point for each time a writer uses passive voice in a submission paper." While other law reviews may not be quite so strict with regard to using active voice, you should play it safe by almost always avoiding passive voice.

Of course, there are instances where it is actually preferable to use passive voice. For example, it may be better to write:

```
Over 500 drivers were pulled over last month.
```

than to write:

```
The police pulled over more than 500 drivers
last month.
```

But such instances are few and far between. Stick to using the active voice almost 100% of the time and your submission paper will be much more readable, and will likely receive a higher score.

g. Choose Your Words Carefully

Mark Twain observed that the difference between the right word and almost the right word is like the difference between lightning and the lightning bug.[1] This is just as true in legal writing as it is in fiction and narrative nonfiction writing, in journalism, and in advertising. The bottom line is that when you are conveying ideas with words on paper, those words matter. And the words you choose not only greatly affect the message you convey, they *are* the message.

Consider the following two examples. They represent two ways of conveying the same information—the general constitutional standard applied to plea bargains—in the introduction section of a submission paper. (Both samples are based on actual submission papers made public by the Georgetown University Law Center; footnotes have been omitted.[2])

Example One:

Because criminal defendants who enter into plea agreements with the government necessarily waive their rights under the U.S. Constitution to a trial by judge or jury, to confront accusers, and to remain silent, special care must be necessarily taken to ensure that such agreements are made voluntarily and intelligently in accordance with the Due Process Clause.

Example Two:

Guilty pleas, which implicate constitutional rights to trial by jury, to confront accusers, and to remain silent, must be voluntary and intelligent.

Example One is awful, is it not? The reason why seems obvious; it says the same thing as Example Two but uses more than twice the number of words. This is a flagrant violation of one of the basic rules of good writing: omit needless words. Shorter is almost always better. But Example One's problems go much deeper than that. It uses not only *more* words, but *more complex* words as well.

i. Prefer simple terms over complex ones

It is commonly known now in the writing-in-plain-English era of legal prose that using legalese is one of the biggest no-no's for lawyers and law students. The reason is that antiquated jargon such as *avers, contends, to wit, aforementioned, whereas, hereinafter*, as well as countless others—not to mention all those ancient Latin phrases—do a poor job of conveying the message the writer is trying to get across. Instead, these unwieldy terms distract.

But this is not limited to legalese. Any term or phrase that can be simplified, while retaining its meaning, should be. Let's look at the examples above. Example One refers to "plea agreements with the government" while Example Two refers to "guilty pleas." Example One says plea bargains must be "made voluntarily and intelligently in accordance with the Due Process Clause" while Example Two says they "must be voluntary and intelligent."

I believe the superiority of how Example Two conveys the same message with simpler (and fewer) words is self-evident. But to just zero in on one specific word choice, let's look at the subtle but powerful difference between "voluntarily" (used in Example One) and "voluntary" (used in Example Two). The former, although it has only two extra letters and one extra syllable, seems to have come from a different planet than the latter. "Voluntarily" is an ugly legalism, a word that exists almost exclusively in ancient court opinions and lazy lawyers' briefs, while "voluntary" is a common word used in everyday English. Always, always, always use the simpler word. Lawyers, judges, and law review graders will get your meaning quicker and reward you accordingly.

ii. Use concrete words and phrases

In your submission paper, as in every persuasive, predictive, or academic piece of legal writing, you are telling the reader a story. You are explaining what happened, what the law is, and how that law should be applied to the facts. It's the kind of story lawyers are trained to tell. Concrete words bring the story to life; they do this by allowing the reader to visualize the events, making it more impactful and memorable. Abstract words, on the other hand, water the story down.

Consider the image conjured up in your mind in response to the words in the left hand column below (which are vague) versus the corresponding words on the right (which are concrete):

vehicle	vs.	1995 red Honda Accord
intersection	vs.	four-way stoplight
four occupants	vs.	family of four

The word "vehicle" gives no clear picture of the vehicle being referred to — car? truck? minivan? SUV? Who knows? By contrast, the words "1995 red Honda Accord" are the equivalent of holding up a color photograph of the car to the reader's face; you cannot help but see it with your mind's eye. Such imagery draws the reader in and makes it far more likely he or she will get (and agree with) what it is you're trying to say.

Using concrete words, particularly in the introduction and statement of facts section, can strengthen a submission paper by helping the reader see what it is you are saying.

iii. Read your writing out loud

Writing advice such as *use simple terms, prefer concrete words, vary the sentence length, use active voice,* and the like, is aimed at the same goal: to improve the sound of your writing. What many of us forget when we sit down to write is that every word has its own sound. That sound is conveyed through the words on the page just as if it were said out loud. That is why when you come across a very strong piece of writing you may notice that it comes across very well when read aloud.

As noted by eminent novelist Ursula K. Le Guin, "The sound of the language is where it all begins and what it all comes back to. The basic elements of language are physical: the noise words make and the rhythm of their relationships."[3] This is just as true in legal writing as it is in any other kind of prose. Yet law students are often not taught to read their writing aloud because the focus in legal writing classes is on other elements of writing, such as structure, clarity, persuasiveness, and use of authorities.

Try this: go back to Example One and Example Two at the beginning of this section (Section g), and read each one of them aloud. You will see that there is a vast difference in not only how each example looks, but also how each one sounds. Example One is clunky, overly wordy, and difficult to follow. Example Two is easy and clear.

This is what is meant by writing in plain English, which lawyers have been encouraged to do for at least forty years. Plain English reads the way we speak, more or less. And so terms such as *shall* and *and/or* have no place in it. No one uses these or any other legalese words when speaking, so you should not use them when writing, unless, of course, they are contained in a quote you use.

There is much more to the sound of writing than what I have touched on here, but, just as with most of the topics I have covered in this book, less is more. For the purpose of the write-on competition, it is enough that you keep in mind that writing should sound good out loud to read well on paper. You will have plenty of time to pore over more sophisticated writing techniques in the future, if that is where your life leads you; your goal for now should be only to write a persuasive and well-supported submission paper, and quickly.

h. Politically Correct (Again)

Just as you should avoid, if at all possible, making a politically unpopular claim in your submission paper, you should also avoid revealing political bias in your writing. Refrain from using emotion- or policy-driven rationale when discussing a politically-charged issue, such as abortion, immigration, or the death penalty. For example, avoid writing that abortion or the death penalty is *good* or *bad*, or *right* or *wrong*. Inserting a personal view may be popular with some graders (i.e., with those who agree with your viewpoint) but is likely to turn other graders off.

I spoke with one law review member who told me about a submission paper she graded where the student clearly revealed through the wording of his paper that he was pro-gun rights. She told me that the student's views just rubbed her the wrong way and made her look more critically at the student's analysis and argument. Although the law reviewer said that her disagreement with the student's viewpoint did not affect the score she assigned to the paper (which, she told me, was low), it is easy to see that rubbing the graders the wrong way is clearly not in your best interest as an applicant for law review.

Indeed, while the graders you impress with your viewpoint probably won't give you extra points, the ones you offend may very well dock you. Accordingly, stick to arguing the law according to the authorities in the source materials, and avoid using language that may draw attention to your particular political leanings.

i. Avoid Humor and Sarcasm

Your tone throughout the submission paper should be clear and confident, but you should not go out on a limb by presuming too much about your audience. This principle extends beyond the political bias realm and includes humor and sarcasm as well. What may be funny to you could be offensive to one of the graders, and you don't want to take that chance by trying to play the clown in your paper. Moreover, even if a grader shares your sense of humor, you risk losing the respect of that grader if he or she feels that your submission paper is not the appropriate forum for your humor.

You should also avoid using sarcasm or condescending language. If the graders get a bad vibe from your writing, it is likely to affect their scoring of your paper. So avoid coming off as presumptuous in your writing and you'll stay on the graders' good side, increasing your chances of getting a high score.

j. Address Counterarguments

One of the most important components of any persuasive legal argument is the acknowledgement and appropriate treatment of all potential counterarguments. Your submission paper is no exception. Since the source materials will likely contain legal support for two or more sides of the issue, it is important that you respond to all negative authority contained therein. Cite it, distinguish it, and move on.

k. Mind the Page Limit

Although it is not critical that you strictly conform your first, or even second, draft to the page limit, keep in mind as you write that you should aim to use all of the pages allowed. If the instructions give you a page limit of ten, you'll want your final submission paper to be ten pages in length. Not nine pages, but ten.

As I graded submission papers, almost everyone used up the page limit. However, there were four submission papers that were around one page shy of the page limit and one paper that was *three* pages short. All five of those papers were missing important legal analysis, and none of them received a passing score. Graders in some other write-on competitions are even less sympathetic. One law review member told me, "If you go over the page limit at my school, we will not even consider the submission."

Nonetheless, developing a legal argument takes up space. One of the biggest challenges in the write-on competition is to try and fit the analysis you develop into the page limit provided. If you find that after finishing a full draft of your paper you are still coming up short of the page limit, take another look at your argument section and look for missing pieces or weaknesses. Ask yourself whether you are addressing all possible counterarguments, and whether you are using all of the sources to their maximum effectiveness.

But don't add words to your paper just for the sake of adding words. Make sure you find out what your paper is missing substantively and insert the missing material where it fits best.

If, however, you go over the page limit, don't sweat it at this point. You'll be able to cut your paper down to the required size later on.

Step 5: *Do the Editing Exercise and Draft Your Personal Statement, if Your Competition Includes These*

After finishing the first draft of your submission paper, you will probably want to take a break from it to clear your mind. This is a good point at which to do a first run-through of the editing exercise or to write a first draft of the personal statement, if your competition includes one of these.

You should complete the editing exercise (which is discussed in greater detail in Chapter 7) at least three times in order to find all of the errors placed by the editors. That means that you should not wait until after you finish the submission paper to start on it. Instead, you should tackle it early in the competition so that you can go back over it several times before the end of the competition.

Likewise, it is important that you polish up your personal statement (which is discussed in greater detail in Chapter 8) well before turning it in. Naturally, you should not wait to make a first draft of it either. Writing a draft early in the competition and reviewing it two or three times before submitting it will help ensure that you write as impressive a personal statement as possible.

MID-COMPETITION REMINDER:

Don't Forget to Re-Read the Instructions Often

It is of absolute paramount importance that you follow the instructions to a T. And the only way to be sure that you are following the instructions precisely is to read them several times, never allowing too many days to go by without referring back to them. By the end of the competition, you should have virtually memorized the instructions from your repetitive reading of them.

Remember, since they take only a short time to read but contain a huge amount of valuable information, it's a good idea for you to read them every day until they become firmly imprinted on your brain.

Step 6: *Revise and Organize Your Paper*

The organization of your paper is very important to your success in the write-on competition. Your goal with regard to organization should be to achieve maximum simplicity and readability. That is, you should make your paper as easy to read as possible while presenting an articulate and persuasive legal argument.

A well-organized paper spoon-feeds the writer's argument to the grader so that he or she can assess the paper with as little effort as possible. Conversely, jumbled and disjointed writing will result in a lower score, regardless of how solid the argument may otherwise be.

Keep in mind that the graders of the submission papers will read through several papers in a single sitting and each grader will probably read through your paper only once. That means that your writing must be well-organized and straightforward. If at all possible, avoid complicated prose. Again, the easier time the graders have following your argument, the higher score you are likely to get.

Accordingly, your first edit or two should focus on the following aspects of improving your paper's organization:

a. Improve the Paper's Uniformity and Flow

As you revise your paper, make sure that it reads smoothly from beginning to end and that it does not change gears in an uncomfortable way at any point. The voice, style, and overall flow of your writing should be substantially similar on each page of the paper.

Editing at this stage necessitates that you view the text of your paper on a macro-level, ensuring uniformity of the flow and tone from the first page to the last. Thus, on your initial editing read-through, it is a good idea to pore over the paper from beginning to end, paying particular attention to how the paper *looks* and *feels*, always keeping in mind that each sentence should lead logically to the next sentence. Similarly, each paragraph should lead to the one that follows it.

As discussed previously, it may also be helpful to read out loud during revision in order to understand how your paper sounds. Hearing your prose spoken out loud will reveal your paper's tone and narrative flow, and may also alert you to awkwardly-written passages you might not have noticed while writing.

Two specific techniques for improving the uniformity and flow of a submission paper are to ensuring you have included topic sentences at the beginning of most paragraphs and double-checking that the paragraphs are properly bridged together. These will be covered in subsections b and c below.

b. Make Sure Most Paragraphs Have a Topic Sentence

A well-organized paragraph supports or develops a single controlling idea, which is expressed in a sentence called the topic sentence. A good topic sentence, usually placed at the beginning of the paragraph, tells the reader what the paragraph is about. By stating the controlling idea, a topic sentence reorients the reader to what will be discussed in that paragraph. This gives the reader—particularly if he or she is in a hurry—an easy roadmap to follow.

This is important, because the easier you make it for the graders to understand your argument and its legal support, the higher grade you will get. In fact, organization is nearly always one of the actual grading categories for submission papers. Accordingly, during revision I strongly advise you double-check your paragraphs' topic sentences to make sure that, one, you have included them, and two, they accurately announce what each paragraph is about.

c. Bridge the Paragraphs Together

Paragraphs must not only be clear and organized individually, but also collectively. They must be connected by transitions. The flow of the paper depends on it.

Think of it this way. Suppose the several ideas you're setting down in the submission paper—e.g., the points of your argument—are islands in the ocean. Some islands are bigger than others. Some are closer to each other, while some may seem to be drifting off, barely even in sight from all the others. Similarly, some ideas are smaller bits of a cohesive whole, while others require a bit more effort to reel in. Your task is to gather these islands into a sort of archipelago kingdom you rule. But to make sure that you have full control over it all, you need to connect the islands to each other. Now, it's fine that each island isn't directly connected to every other island, especially when they're far enough away from each other to not really be related at all. But ultimately you want all the islands connected to comprise a unified whole. So what do you do?

You build bridges.

In writing your submission paper, these bridges are your transitions. You have two ideas that are related—islands close enough that you can build a bridge between them—but ultimately distinct. In order to help your readers across that gulf, then, you need to put in a transition.

Note: Though most paragraphs should have a topic sentence, there are situations when a paragraph might not need one. Examples include where a paragraph narrates a series of events or continues developing an idea you introduced (with a topic sentence) in the previous paragraph. The vast majority of submission paper paragraphs, however, should have a topic sentence.

The topic sentence is a great place to do this. Ideally, the topic sentence should not only announce what the paragraph is about, but also connect the material that preceded it with what follows. One brief example should suffice here.

Suppose in one paragraph you argue that a city ordinance which bans certain yard signs directly advances the asserted governmental interest, and you begin the next paragraph with the following sentence: "In addition, the ordinance is no more extensive than necessary to serve the governmental interest." Here, the reference to "the ordinance" echoes back to the ordinance discussed in the prior paragraph. And the transition *'in addition'* clearly establishes the continuation of legal analysis flowing from the prior paragraph. That, dear readers, is a masterful bridge.

Following is a list of strong transition words and phrases (to bridge not only paragraphs, but also sentences), which could be helpful as you write your submission paper[4]:

- **When adding a point:** and, also, in addition, besides, what is more, similarly, nor, along with, likewise, too, moreover, further
- **When giving an example:** for instance, for example, as one example, to cite but one example, for one thing, for another thing, likewise, another
- **When contrasting:** but, yet, instead, however, on the one hand, on the other hand, still, nevertheless, nonetheless, conversely, on the contrary, whereas, in contrast to
- **When comparing:** similarly, likewise, in the same way
- **When restating:** in other words, that is, this means, in similar terms, in short, put differently, again
- **When pressing a point:** in fact, as a matter of fact, indeed, of course, without exception, still, even so

- **When summing up:** to summarize, to sum up, to conclude, in conclusion, in short, in brief, so, and so, consequently, therefore, all in all
- **When sequencing ideas:** First, … Second, … Third, … Finally, …

d. Make Sure There Is Consistency of Argument

You should also watch out for inconsistencies in your argument. Make sure that your paper says $A+B+C = ABC$, and not $A+B+C = ABD$.

One law review member I interviewed told me that he read through so many disjointed arguments in the submission papers that they were the rule rather than the exception in the competition at his school. This is no surprise considering that, on account of the time pressures, students often get to writing so quickly that their analysis breaks down (unbeknownst to them) at some point while they're typing away at top speed. But such mistakes are easy to fix as long as they are caught on time.

Focus on reviewing your argument both structurally and substantively during the first couple of edits. This will help ensure that your argument is not only logical but also solid, if not airtight.

e. Avoid Redundancy

Unnecessary repetition can jeopardize your paper in two ways. First, it unnecessarily uses up the precious little space you are allotted to formulate a persuasive legal argument. Every redundant sentence you include in your paper takes a sentence away from the legal analysis that should be included in your paper.

Second, graders tend to view redundancy in submission papers as a waste of their time. After reading through dozens of submission papers on end, graders become very adept at locating and focusing on the legal argument in each paper. So when they come across a paragraph of background or analysis that they had already read earlier in the paper, they often feel that reading that portion of the paper is time wasted.

Thus, you should focus on eliminating unnecessary repetition during your first edit or two. This will help keep you on the graders' good side while opening up space for the rest of your argument and helping you to conform to the page limit.

f. Adhere to the Page Limit

At this point you should begin editing down (or adding to) your paper in order to ensure that you use up all (but not more than) the number of pages allowed. Above, I mentioned that you need not think too much about the page limit in your first draft. But now that you have finished a full-length draft and you are at the revising/organizing stage, you should focus on conforming your paper to the page limit.

If you're over the page limit, try first cutting out any additional unnecessary repetitious material from your paper. Next, try and cut individual sentences and/or paragraphs from your paper, or combining them in order to save space. You still want to try and keep your paragraphs and sentences relatively short, but if combining them can save you significant space without making the text too bulky, then you should go ahead and do it.

Finally, if you are still over the page limit, determine which sections of your paper are more important and which are less so (e.g., which counterarguments are more important to address than others). You may need to delete entire sections if you cannot get your paper down to the required size, but you must avoid removing portions that are essential to your argument. Keep in mind that if you submit a paper that exceeds the page limit, you risk at a minimum, losing *major* points with the graders. Or your paper may even be categorically eliminated from the competition.

If you're under the page limit, you are almost assuredly missing important legal analysis. Go back through the source materials and make sure that you have used all the supporting authority and that you have addressed all negative authority as well. If your argument seems solid and you've exhausted the source materials, think up counterarguments that you have not yet touched on and address each of them, making sure to state why they do not prevail over your claim.

One law review member I spoke with told me that her advice to students in the write-on competition was for them to simply "walk away" from the paper if they ran up against a problem. She said that whenever she was stuck on an issue while writing her submission paper, she simply took a break by engaging in some completely un-related activity, such as going for a run or going to a movie. Then, with her mind cleared from the stress of the competition, she would usually realize what her analysis was missing.

g. Save the Deleted Material

When editing text out of your paper, paste it into another file in order to have it handy in case you decide to re-add it later on. Also, maintaining a "deleted material" file will help you overcome some of the hesitation you may feel about letting go of relevant but unneces-sary material.

h. Include an Introduction and a Conclusion

You should include a brief paragraph at the beginning and end of your paper that summarizes your argument, whether or not the in-structions call for it. The introduction will help the graders under-stand your argument and the conclusion will remind them of why your argument prevails. Also, including these two sections will im-prove the overall readability of your paper and make it look more professional.

Step 7: *Proofread*

Once you have revised and organized your paper, give it a very close proofread, making sure "principal" is not supposed to be "prin-ciple," and so on. Good spelling, punctuation, and grammar are im-mensely critical since errors of these types tend to jump off the page and distract the grader.

Once these types of errors are detected in your paper, the grader is more likely to look closely for others — in the grader's mind, if you misspelled "principle," you most likely made other mistakes too. And when graders look hard for errors, they tend to find them. So proofread carefully and try to polish your writing to the point of near grammatical and spelling perfection.

As you proofread, make sure to focus on the following areas:

a. Citations, Including Case Names

It is easy for you, as the writer, to overlook misspellings in case names or other citation-related errors. But graders will notice any such mistakes immediately. This is because graders' repetitive reading of submission papers results in them having all the source names imprinted on their brains. So, pay particular attention to case titles to make sure "Smith v. Jones" is not actually supposed to read "Smyth v. Jones, Inc."

Also, double-check that the citations themselves are accurate. For example, it is not uncommon to insert an "F.3d" where an "F.2d" should be, and make sure that citations to the Second and Third circuit courts of appeal read "2d" and "3d," respectively (not "2nd" and "3rd"). The best way to go about doing this is to use one of your editing read-throughs to concentrate exclusively on citations. That way you can ensure that your citations are accurate and correctly written, and you can then concentrate on editing other aspects of your paper.

Note: Do not rely on the spell-checking features of Microsoft Word or of any other program. Those features will fail to highlight where you have spelled a word correctly, but it's the wrong word to use in that instance, such as forth/fourth, whether/weather, and concede/conceit.

One particular area where some students get into trouble is the difference between writing the case name in the body of the paper and in a footnote. Ignoring the difference can cost you major points in the competition. Remember that while case names in the body text should be italicized, case names in footnotes must not be, unless: 1) you are giving a partial case name; or 2) you are giving the case name in full, but without a citation.

Again, you must adhere precisely to the Bluebook or other citation manual recommended by your school (see Preparation Activity #3 in Chapter 5, above), as well as any instructions regarding citations.

b. Quotes

Graders have been known to scrutinize quoted text in submission papers very closely. This is not surprising when you consider that one of the regular duties of law review editors is to ensure that every quote in a submitted legal article is perfectly accurate. Thus, you should make sure that your quotes reflect exactly what the quoted passage states, using the Bluebook (or other citation manual recommended at your school) to guide you in how to correctly make alterations to the quoted text.

c. Footnotes and Endnotes

Don't forget to edit the text in the footnotes or endnotes in addition to the text in the body. Just because they are written in smaller font doesn't mean the errors will go unnoticed. Assume the grader will read every word on every page you write, and edit every sentence and citation to perfection accordingly.

There are some Bluebook rules regarding footnotes and endnotes that you should pay close attention to. For example, you should review Bluebook Rule 10.9 on internal short cites. Under that rule, you may only use the short cite of a previously-cited case if you cited the case: 1) in the same general textual discussion; or 2) within one of the preceding five footnotes. If you cited the case in footnote 25, do not short cite it in footnote 31.

Other Bluebook rules important to review with regard to footnotes and endnotes are Rules 3.5 (on internal cross references), 4.1 (on short cites), and 4.2 (on the use of *supra* and *hereinafter*). These rules can be tricky. Note that you can only use *id.* if the preceding footnote has only one case in it.

Also note the proper form for a *supra* cite, which you will use primarily when citing a law review article.

Example: *See* Jones, *supra* note 43, at 228.

Using the *supra* citation form is much easier than giving the whole cite again.

Finally, it will be helpful to review Bluebook Rules 1.2 (on signals) and 1.3 (on order of signals). Although there is no need for you to get fancy with your use of signals, you may want to throw in a *Compare ... with ...* cite somewhere. And remember that proper use of signals is very important.

d. Style and Structure

Because of the competition time-crunch, many students commit stylistic and structural errors that they otherwise might not have made. It is important, then, to keep these easily-overlooked areas in mind as you write and edit your paper.

First, do not forget about IRAC. This acronym (standing for Issue, Rule, Analysis, and Conclusion) is a guiding principle throughout your first year of law school. So keep it in mind — and use it! — while writing your submission paper.

Next, remember to synthesize the legal authorities. Do not simply scribble down a laundry list of court holdings or legislative provisions. You need to put them together and come up with a workable rule. Also, it is important that you adequately apply the legal authorities to the facts. You can do this by providing a thorough fact-by-fact comparison. Leaving relevant facts out of your legal analysis could cost you major points.

And speaking of facts, for some reason, some students exclude material facts from the background section. This is a big mistake. As mentioned above, you must include all legally significant facts and any other necessary facts in the background section.

Finally, one small detail students often slip up on is the choice of verb used to describe a court's action. Remember, there is a difference between "holds," "concludes," "reasons," "finds," "decides," "recognizes," "adopts," and "states." You should not write that the court "holds" unless the asserted point is actually part of the court's holding. Also, you should never state that a court "feels" or "believes" something. Stick with the traditional and assertive language discussed above.

e. Your Paper's Title

One detail that many students leave out is the title. But this seemingly minor omission can cost you major points. Putting a title at the head of the paper helps the grader know what to expect before they read the first sentence. This makes their job easier and your paper can only benefit from such an inclusion.

Keep in mind, however, that not every type of legal document you may be asked to write lends itself well to having a title, though most do. For example, if you are asked to write an "essay" or an "article," it goes without saying that having a title at the top is recommended. Likewise, if you are asked to write a legal memorandum, you should include the issue in the "RE" line and include a title stating your overarching legal claim above the introduction. (Step 8, below, discusses how to handle being asked to write specific legal documents in the write-on competition.)

Note: If adding a title would be contrary to the instructions, then obviously don't do it. Keep in mind that the instructions are not suggestions. They must be scrupulously followed, regardless of the advice in this book or from any other source.

Step 8: *Maximize Your Paper's Aesthetic Quality*

Perhaps the single most important aspect of submission papers that writers frequently overlook is the overall appearance of the finished product. All too often, students revise and proofread their papers for hours on end, only to submit a paper that looks unappealing and unprofessional.

Several law review members I spoke with told me that they were surprised at the high number of submission papers they graded that looked more like rough drafts than final copies. As a result of the numerous unprofessional-looking submissions, writers who submit clean and refined papers have a clear advantage in the write-on competition.

Once again, it is helpful to keep in mind that the graders read through dozens of submission papers relatively quickly. This is because they are usually under time pressures to grade the papers and return them to the law review office. Thus, their first impression of your paper — which is established within a second or two of picking it up and glancing at the first page — has a strong influence on the grade they end up assigning the paper. In any event, even if they do not judge your paper on its appearance consciously, they will almost assuredly do it subconsciously. It's human nature.

I think this is the one area where you can improve your paper the most with the least amount of work. You can do so by skimming over your paper and making sure that it is professional in appearance and pleasant to look at, while conforming precisely to the instructions.

As you review your submission paper for aesthetic quality, keep in mind the following issues:

a. Which Legal Document?

One way to go the extra mile in making your paper stand out aesthetically from other submission papers is to make it look (at least somewhat) like the type of legal document you are asked to create. For example, if you are asked to write a "memorandum to the supervising partner," you should add a brief memorandum heading to the first page, including the title of the person you are writing to, an anonymous identity for yourself, the date of the submission deadline, and the problem presented in the prompt. It should look something like this:

```
To:    Supervising Attorney

From:  Associate Attorney

Date:  May 22, 2016

Re:    Derivative Asylum for the Parents of an
       Asylee
```

Make sure that you *do not* include your name or any other identifying information, since such a disclosure may disqualify you from the write-on competition.

Similarly, if the problem says that you are a judicial law clerk and must write an opinion and order for your judge, you should include the title "Opinion and Order" at the top of the first page. Graders appreciate these little details and often use them as a way of separating good papers from great ones. Just make sure you know the precise type of legal document you are being asked to write and make a few small adjustments to make your paper resemble that type of document.

b. Headings

Make sure your headings are not either distractingly long or pathetically short. Each heading should advance your argument, as discussed in Chapter 6, Step 4, above. Read through your headings to make sure that they adequately explain your entire argument without looking at the body text.

None of the headings should take up more than two lines of text, and ideally should consist of only one line. It is also important that headings be in bold typeface, so as to make them stand out from the body text.

Additionally, check to see if any of the headings ended up at the bottom of a page during your revising and editing. If so, find a way to either bump the heading onto the next page or to delete prior text in order to pull the first couple of lines from the next page up under the heading so as to avoid leaving it hanging alone there without any text directly underneath.

c. Body Text and Footnotes/Endnotes

Flip through the pages of your paper, scanning them for overall aesthetic appeal. As you do so, ask yourself:

- Are the paragraphs an appropriate length?
- Do the footnotes/endnotes look sharp and polished?
- Does the overall paper look like a professionally-written legal article?

It is important that your paper is professional-looking from beginning to end.

d. Use a Laser Printer

When you finally finish writing your submission paper, make sure you print out the final copy or copies on a laser printer rather than an ink-based one. The sharp, clear finish that laser printing gives to printed pages leaves them looking more professional and of high-quality. Ink printers, on the other hand, sometimes leave pages blurry or with smudge marks. The sleek finish provided by a laser printer gives your paper just one more small advantage over other papers. And every little benefit helps.

The importance of an aesthetically-pleasing final product cannot be overemphasized. Much of the graders' opinion of your paper will be judged in one way or another by its appearance—especially during the two-second glance they will make across the front page just before they begin to read.

Step 9: *Do a Final Proofread Before Submitting Your Paper*

It is often the case that the difference between those who make law review and those who do not is very small, and correcting minor avoidable errors can make all the difference. And whereas your *argument* must only be "solid," your *spelling, grammar,* and *punctuation* should be flawless. You cannot afford to misspell "judgement" or leave out a necessary comma. Also, pay close attention to your cross-references to other footnotes (i.e., with "*supra*" and "*infra*"), as these can become mismatched as a result of adding and deleting footnotes throughout the writing process. Try and reserve a few hours near the end of the competition to go back over your paper with fresh eyes in order to catch any small mistakes you may have overlooked earlier.

Most write-on competitions forbid students from receiving assistance from anyone else. If that is the case, as with every other part of the instructions and the rules for your law school's competition, do exactly as they say. If, however, your write-on competition allows others to edit your work, by all means, take advantage of that liberty and get someone to read over your submission paper. Having others' input on your writing can improve your submission paper immensely, and you should do so if permitted.

Chapter 7

The Editing Exercise

In order to perform well on the editing exercise, you will need to go through and complete it at least three times. This is necessary because these tests tend to contain a great quantity of errors, many of which are very difficult to find. For that reason, it is important that you complete the editing exercise once early in the competition—such as after you complete the first draft of your submission paper—and repeat it at least two more times before the competition deadline.

Keep the following suggestions in mind as you complete the editing exercise:

1. Follow the Instructions

As is the case with writing your submission paper, you must follow the instructions precisely in order to succeed in the editing exercise. Some instructions, for example, include specific editing symbols that they expect you to use (e.g., for deleting or moving text). You should default to those symbols over any others, even over those appearing in writing style guides such as the Chicago Manual of Style.

2. If the Editing Exercise Is Paper-Based ...

If your editing exercise is given to you in printed form, be sure to make several photocopies of it before putting your pen to the paper. That way, you can use a clean copy on which to make the final edits in order to turn in a polished and error-free copy.

Another reason to make copies is to be able to undertake the editing exercise from scratch more than once. This method of completing the exercise is highly recommendable if you have the time to do so, because it helps you find errors that you may have overlooked the first time around. If you merely go back over the test that you already completed, you will likely repeat the mistakes made on the prior test because you have already written them down.

If you do take several separate tests, synthesize them at the end of the competition so that your final product reflects all of the errors you found and corrected.

Another good idea is to use a fine-point red ink pen while making your edits. The fine-point will write more clearly in the small font footnotes or endnotes that you may be editing, and the color red will help your writing stand out from the black printed text. Finally, it is recommendable that you have whiteout on hand. It's very easy to make mistakes while writing your edits onto the page, and it is much easier to blot a little whiteout onto the page than to start over from scratch on a whole new piece of paper.

3. If the Editing Exercise Is Computer-Based ...

If your editing exercise is given to you on the computer, try changing the zoom to 200% or more in order to be able to see very well what you're doing. The footnotes you're assigned to correct may very well be in a minute font size and zooming in can illuminate errors you may not have otherwise found. Plus, it will help you see just what you are doing to the text so as to avoid making unintended changes.

4. Try to Find an Error in Every Footnote

If you find a footnote that appears to contain no errors whatsoever, take another look at it. It is very rare for editors to include flawless footnotes in an editing exercise. So when you see a seemingly perfect footnote, you should feel like you've missed something rather than feeling relief for having come across an apparently flawless footnote. Don't spend all day agonizing over a footnote where you see no errors, but do review it carefully to make sure you did not miss something.

5. Don't Get Comfortable after Making a Few Edits

After making several corrections to a footnote, do not become complacent and assume that there are not more errors to be found. Students tend to move on to the next footnote after making a few edits, without methodically going through each component of each citation and scrutinizing it from all possible angles. This is a dangerous practice and may result in your missing some of the errors.

It is best to separate each component of each citation in each footnote into its own separate entity to be analyzed individually. Make sure to check the signal, the case name (for spelling and format), the page number, reporter or digest, and the parenthetical (for spelling and grammar). This is where your bluebooking skills must be put on display in full force.

6. Insert Notes If Allowed

Some competitions allow students to write notes in the margins of the editing exercise to explain a specific edit. You should do this whenever you're not sure about the change you are making. If you cannot decide which rule to apply in order to fix a particular error, add a notation explaining why you chose the rule you did. This will signal to the grader that you put some thought into the choice you made, and that you recognize that choosing the rule you did was a close call.

7. If You Don't Know It, Look It Up

Use the index of the Bluebook to help find the answer to any editing questions you may have. Although it is often criticized for its lack of user-friendliness, the Bluebook's index can usually—though not always—point you in the right direction of where to find the answer you are looking for.

Also, keep in mind that the Bluebook does not always cover *every* edit you must make. Sometimes you may have to synthesize rules. When you do so, it is helpful to include explanatory notes along with your edits.

Chapter 8

The Personal Statement

If your school's write-on competition requires you to write a personal statement, treat it as an opportunity to convey your likeable personality and interesting background. Keep in mind that it is not necessarily important that you have a likeable personality or an interesting background. What is important is how you portray yourself through your writing. In addition, the personal statement is your chance to show off your writing skills.

Here are some suggestions for writing a successful personal statement:

1. Follow the Directions

No big surprise here; you must follow the directions in order to write a successful personal statement. For example, if the instructions ask you to write about, say, 'why you want to be on law review' or 'why you came to law school,' address these specific topics. After you finish writing the personal statement, re-read the instructions to make sure that you followed them precisely.

2. Write Well

Make sure that your writing is intelligent and interesting, and flawless with regard to grammar, spelling, and punctuation. This is your opportunity to show what kind of a writer you are outside of the confines of the submission paper. Use it well. Write something that the graders will find interesting, but keep it simple.

As is the case with the submission paper, repetitive editing is key to polishing your prose in the personal statement. After you write a rough draft, leave it alone for a day or two, and come back to it later on to do the editing. Repeat this at least two or three times, making sure that with each edit, you are improving the paper substantively, aesthetically, and grammatically.

3. Portray Yourself as Interesting and Likeable

Try to emphasize your experiences and attributes that make you stand out from the crowd, such as traveling to exotic countries or working at a unique job. But don't just make a laundry list of your purported "interesting" qualities. Tell a story or find another way to convey the information in an otherwise entertaining way.

But avoid casting yourself in a manner that might rub the readers the wrong way. Don't be conceited about your accomplishments and avoid highlighting positions or experiences that might paint you in a politically ideological light. Strive instead to sound humble and politically open-minded.

4. A Note on Specialty Journal Personal Statements

Some specialty journals require applicants to write a personal statement geared specifically toward their journal. If this is the case in your write-on competition, draw upon your background, your experiences, and any other factors that may exist that evidence your interest in that journal's particular topic (whether it be international law, constitutional law, patent law, or whatever).

For example, if a specialty journal dealing exclusively with international law asks journal applicants to write a personal statement specifically for their journal, you would be well-advised to emphasize any experience you have living, studying, visiting, or even researching a foreign country. It would also be beneficial to include any foreign language abilities you may possess or any other connection you may have to a foreign country or to international law.

5. Have Someone Review Your Personal Statement, If Allowed

As mentioned above, most law schools do not allow students to receive outside assistance during the write-on competition. If, however, your write-on competition allows others to edit your work, you should get someone to read over your personal statement, since having others review your work is a great way to improve your written product.

Conclusion

Students who familiarize themselves with the write-on competition and develop an organized plan of how to tackle it are much more likely to succeed in the competition and get onto their school's law review. After reading this book, you should now be more familiar with how the competition works, how to prepare for it, and how to write a winning submission paper. In addition, if you implement the techniques discussed in this book, it should help you improve your performance in the write-on competition.

Remember, you will be able to achieve your goals with or without the law review credential and, conversely, being on law review guarantees you nothing. The real key to success is sustained hard work and a long-term dedication to achieving your goals. The law review credential is just one factor of many in determining where your legal career leads you.

Perhaps the most important piece of advice to pass along to you is this: Relax and don't lose sight of how fortunate you are to be getting a legal education in the first place. A law degree in and of itself is a prestigious distinction, worthy of praise.

So don't drive yourself crazy over the write-on competition. You should approach it with the confidence of knowing what to expect, and with the knowledge that whether or not you make law review does not define who you are as a lawyer or as a person. The write-on competition is just that; a competition. You should take it and its results with a grain of salt.

Now that you're ready for the write-on competition, there's only one last thing to tell you:

GOOD LUCK!

Afterword

A few years ago, back when I practiced at a law firm in California, a summer associate entered my office without knocking and took a seat in one of the two chairs in front of my desk. She sat there silently for a few seconds, smiling at me. But she wasn't just smiling—she was beaming. I smiled back because it was all I could do. I had no idea why she had come into my office and I racked my brain, trying to remember if I had given her a research project or a writing assignment.

"I made it onto law review," she blurted out.

I rose from my chair and extended my hand, congratulating her and telling her how excited I was for her, which I was. How could I not be? I knew what a big deal it was, how big of an impact making law review has on a young lawyer-to-be's life.

She shook my hand and sat back down. We both did. Then she added: "And I would never have gotten on if it wasn't for your book."

It surprises me every time, though of course by now it shouldn't. Every summer the annual ritual repeats itself; in June and July I receive dozens of thank you messages in my email inbox from law students who have just made law review or another law journal at their school, and occasionally I am treated to an in-person expression of gratitude as well. I keep every one of those emails in a folder on my computer. And every summer I get another bundle of them.

Since I wrote this book over the course of a few months in 2007, it has taken on a life of its own. It is now, according to my research, stocked in nearly every U.S. law library,[1] as well as a number of law libraries abroad, and is on recommended reading lists for first-year students at law schools across the country—at New York Law

School,[2] the University of Texas School of Law,[3] and the University of Wisconsin Law School,[4] to name just a few. There are thousands of copies of *Making Law Review* in print and every summer, like clockwork, I receive another bundle of thank you emails.

But the reactions to my book have not been universally positive. Some, I have learned, quite simply detest it. One reviewer on Amazon.com, for instance, who gave this book a one-star rating, wrote:

> It takes a lot of devoted time and effort to write on to a journal. Reading this book did not help at all. This book offers no secrets or helpful strategies.[5]

The reviewer, I have to admit, was mostly right. It does take a lot of devoted time and effort to write on to a journal. And this book, it is true, does not offer any "secrets." (The only "secret" to excelling in the write-on competition is to write a great submission paper, which is no secret at all.) I would also concede that the strategies outlined in the book—and here I must disagree with the reviewer; the book does offer numerous helpful strategies—are all ones law students should be aware of already or could likely find in another resource.

It's all true. And yet, less than three weeks ago I received an email message from a law student named Joshua Reid who told me:

> I'm a member of the Law Review thanks to you.... Every time a 1L asks me about getting on a journal, I refer them to your book. 'Just read it,' I tell them. 'If you don't get on a journal after reading that book, it wasn't meant to be.' And I believe it.

I receive testimonials like this every year. One reviewer on Amazon.com, Harry Dixon, who gave the book five stars, called the book "Essential reading for anyone serious about the write-on competition."[6] The positive reviews and testimonials over the years have been an avalanche when compared with the trickle of critical voices. So yes, it is true the book offers no "secrets," but, even so, year after year dozens of law students swear this book gave them a significant advantage in the write-on competition. How can that be?

The answer, I think, is in the eye of the beholder. An advice book is only as helpful as the reader makes it. Returning to that one-starred reviewer's comment reveals precisely the problem, or, if you will, the misunderstanding; he or she claimed that "reading this book did not help at all." To which I would respond, How could reading *any* book help? Reading, by itself, accomplishes nothing. For instance, reading the Contracts casebook cover to cover will not get you an A on the Contracts final. Just like reading an LSAT prep book would not have guaranteed you a high score on that exam. If a student wants to make it onto a journal in law school, he or she must get top grades and/or excel in the write-on competition; reading this or any other book is only useful to the extent it helps the student to accomplish one or both of these things. Competition graders do not care what books, if any, a candidate has read; only the submission paper matters, along with, if applicable, the editing exam and personal statement.

This book is not a shortcut. I do not believe there is a shortcut for the write-on competition. However, can this book give you an edge? I believe it can, and the testimonials bear that out. But only if you *use* it rather than just *read* it.

Something I said a few pages ago in the Conclusion is worth repeating here: don't drive yourself crazy over the write-on competition. Keep it all in perspective. Life is not about accomplishments or accolades. In my personal opinion, there is far too much anxiety and pressure in the legal profession already, beginning in law school, followed by the bar exam and continuing through the practice of law. It is not my aim here to add to the stress. Only to present information students can use to do as well as possible in one very narrow sliver of the law school experience: the write-on competition. That's it.

My supervising partner at that California firm I mentioned earlier once told me to think of law practice as a marathon, not a sprint. He was right. But his advice applies much more broadly than to just law practice; life, too, is a long-haul journey. The longest one any of us will ever take. Before you know it, law school will be a distant memory. And if you're lucky you'll only remember the good parts. It is not about making law review, in other words; it is about following your passion and living the life you want. It is about the journey.

I wish you the best of luck on yours. May it be a long and happy one.

Wes Henricksen
Miami, Florida

Appendix

Here are the answers to the Bluebooking Quiz beginning on page 45. Each of the entries below explains which part of the citation contains an error and where in the Bluebook (20th ed.) the rule can be found addressing the topic. The corrected version of each citation follows the explanation of the errors. (Where information was missing from the original citation, it has been filled in with generic material to serve as an example of—but not necessarily the only—right answer.)

Footnote 1: 5 errors

- First names should not be used in case name [Rule 10.2.1(g)]
- "Versus" in the case name is abbreviated as "v." [Rule 10]
- There is no space in "F.2d" [Rule 10; Table T.1]
- Citation is missing a pinpoint cite [Rule 10]
- The Third Circuit Court of Appeals is abbreviated "3d Cir.," not "3rd Cir." [Rule 10.4; Rule 10.6]

Written correctly, the citation should be:

[1] *Ramirez v. Boudreaux*, 322 F.2d 25, 29 (3d Cir. 1996).

Footnote 2: 1 error

- Citation is missing the subsection symbols, "§§" [Rule 3.3(b)]

Written correctly, the citation should be:

[2] 29 U.S.C. §§ 1902–1911 (2007).

Footnote 3: 5 errors

- First names should not be used in case name [Rule 10.2.1(g)]
- "United States" should not be abbreviated in this instance [Rule 10.2.1(f)]

- Citation missing reporter volume number [Rule 10; Rule 10.3.2]
- Citations to the reporter Federal Supplement 2d should contain spaces between the abbreviations, such as: "F. Supp. 2d" [Table T.1]
- Citation is missing a pinpoint cite [Rule 10]

Written correctly, the citation should be:

³ *Tolosa v. United States*, 195 F. Supp. 2d 88, 91 (S.D. Cal. 2005).

Footnote 4: 4 errors

- "Publishing" should be abbreviated as "Publ'g" [Table T.6]
- Note: It is proper to include "City of" in a case name [Rule 10.2.1(f)]
- Citation is missing a pinpoint cite [Rule 10]
- The First Circuit Court of Appeals is abbreviated "1st Cir.," not "CA1" [Rule 10.4; Rule 10.6]
- Citation is missing a parenthetical [Rule 1.2]

Written correctly, the citation should be:

⁴ *See also United Colonies Publ'g v. City of Spokane*, 153 F.3d 441, 450 (1st Cir. 2006) (holding that a business visa cannot be issued solely on the basis of an employment contract).

Footnote 5: 2 errors

- The title should be italicized instead of underlined [Rule 16.3]
- The Harvard Law Review is abbreviated "HARV. L. REV." [Table T.13]

Written correctly, the citation should be:

⁵ Natalia Salgado, *Immigration Inconsistencies: The Circuit Split on Fiancée Visas*, 115 HARV. L. REV. 88, 95 (2002).

Footnote 6: 5 errors

- "Construction" should be abbreviated as "Constr." [Table T.6]
- "West" should be abbreviated as "W." [Table T.6]
- "Ireland" should be abbreviated as "Ir." [Table T.10.3]
- Citations to the reporter Federal Supplement should contain spaces between the abbreviations, such as: "F. Supp." [Table T.1]

- Citation is missing a pinpoint cite [Rule 10]

Written correctly, the citation should be:

⁶ *Wade Constr., Inc. v. W. Wynn Mfg. of Ir.*, 82 F. Supp. 233, 245 (D.P.R. 1982).

Footnote 7: 2 errors

- Citations to the Rocky Mountain Mineral Law Institute should contain spaces between the abbreviated terms, such as "Rocky Mtn. Min. L. Inst." [Table T.13.1]
- Citation is missing a parenthetical [Rule 1.2]

Written correctly, the citation should be:

⁷ *See* Robert Evans, *Property Acquisitions in Mineral Exploration*, 37 Rocky Mtn. Min. L. Inst. 581, 599 (1983).

Footnote 8: 3 errors

- The California Reporter should be abbreviated as "Cal. Rptr." [Table T.1]
- There should be no period after "2d" [Table T.1]
- Citation is missing a pinpoint cite [Rule 10]

Written correctly, the citation should be:

⁸ *Hugo v. Thomas*, 221 Cal. Rptr. 2d 393, 401 (Cal. Ct. App. 1993).

Footnote 9: 3 errors

- "H.R. Rep." should be written in small caps [Rule 13]
- The phrase "available at" should be expressed as "reprinted in" [Rule 13.6]
- "Legislative History of the Internal Revenue Act" should be written in small caps [Rule 13.6]

Written correctly, the citation should be:

⁹ H.R. Rep. No. 88-702, at 43 (1954), *reprinted in* 2 NLRB, Legislative History of the Internal Revenue Act, 1954, at 162 (1955).

Footnote 10: 3 errors

- The title of the convention should not be underlined [Rule 21]

- The names of the parties to the agreement should be abbreviated as "U.S." and "Arg." [Rule 21.4.2; Table T.10.3]
- The names of the parties to the agreement shall appear in alphabetical order. [Rule 21.4.2]

Written correctly, the citation should be:

[10] Convention for the Agreement on Free Trade, Aug. 22, 2004, Arg.-U.S., 46 U.S.T. 1184.

Endnotes

Introduction

1. This statement deserves some clarification. It is true that, for me, the law review credential has been instrumental in opening many doors. But my experience is not universal. I have worked alongside many law clerks, attorneys, and law professors who were never on law review, or on any journal for that matter, who are not only smarter than me, but also more successful. I have also known many former law review members who have struggled to try and break into the career track they desired; I, myself, fit into this category of job-seekers for years. I guess what I want to get across is that while the law review credential is helpful, it does not determine anyone's destiny. It is just one of many factors employers look at.

Chapter 1

1. First-year members of the Barry Law Review, for instance, are called "Associate Editors." See, e.g., Spring 2016 Barry Law Review Masthead, Vol. 21, Issue 2.

2. The Michigan Law Review's webpage, http://www.michiganlawreview .org, accessed on Oct. 10, 2016.

3. The Washington Law Review's webpage, http://www.law.washington .edu/WLR, accessed on Oct. 10, 2016.

4. The University of Pennsylvania Law Review's webpage, http://www .pennumbra.com, accessed on Oct. 10, 2016.

5. The Harvard Law Review's webpage, http://www.harvardlawreview .org, accessed on Oct. 10, 2016.

6. The Yale Law Journal's webpage, http://www.thepocketpart.org, accessed on Oct. 10, 2016.

7. The Columbia Law Review's webpage, http://www.columbialawreview .org, accessed on Oct. 10, 2016.

8. The Michigan Law Review's webpage, http://www.michiganlawreview
.org, accessed on Oct. 10, 2016.

9. Charles E. Hughes, *Forward*, 50 Yale L. J. 737, 737 (1941) (quoting Holmes).

10. Erwin N. Griswold, *The Harvard Law Review—Glimpses of Its History as Seen by an Aficionado* (1987).

11. Frederick C. Hicks, *Materials and Methods of Legal Research* 207 (3rd ed. 1942).

12. Barbara H. Cane, *The Role of Law Review in Legal Education*, 31 J. Leg. Ed. 215, 220 n.32 (1981).

13. John J. McKelvey, *The Law School Review, 1887–1937*, 50 Harv. L. Rev. 868, 868 (1937).

14. William M. Landes & Richard A. Posner, *The Economic Structure of Intellectual Property Law* 3 (Belknap Press 2003).

15. The information contained in this chart was synthesized from several sources: Frederick C. Hicks, *Materials and Methods of Legal Research* 207 (3rd ed. 1942); Barbara H. Cane, *The Role of Law Review in Legal Education*, 31 J. Leg. Ed. 215, 220 n.32 (1981); Geoffrey Preckshot, *All Hail Emperor Law Review: Criticism of the Law Review System and its Success at Provoking Change*, 55 Mo. L. Rev. 1005, 1009 n.25. (1990); Law School Admission Council, *The Official Guide to U.S. Law Schools* (1995); Law School Admission Council, *The Official Guide to ABA-Approved Law Schools* (2002); Law School Admission Council, *The Official Guide to ABA-Approved Law Schools* (2008).

16. *Foreword*, 1 Minn. L. Rev. 63, 64 (1917).

17. *Quoted in* John J. McKelvey, *The Law School Review, 1887–1937*, 50 Harv. L. Rev. 868, 869 (1937).

18. *See, e.g.*, Afton Dekanal, *Faculty-Edited Law Reviews: Should the Law Schools Join the Rest of Academe?*, 57 UMKC L. Rev. 233, 235 (1989).

19. *See, e.g.*, John Paul Jones, *In Praise of Student-Edited Law Reviews: A Reply to Professor Dekanal*, 57 UMKC L. Rev. 241, 244 (1989).

20. Law Review—Wikipedia, the free encyclopedia, http://en.wikipedia
.org/wiki/Law_review, accessed on Nov. 19, 2016.

21. Law Review—Wikipedia, the free encyclopedia, http://en.wikipedia
.org/wiki/Law_review, accessed on Nov. 19, 2016.

22. Law Review—Wikipedia, the free encyclopedia, http://en.wikipedia
.org/wiki/Law_review, accessed on Nov. 19, 2016.

23. Law Review—Wikipedia, the free encyclopedia, http://en.wikipedia
.org/wiki/Law_review, accessed on Oct. 10, 2016.

24. Law Review—Wikipedia, the free encyclopedia, http://en.wikipedia .org/wiki/Law_review, accessed on Oct. 10, 2016.

25. Law Review—Wikipedia, the free encyclopedia, http://en.wikipedia .org/wiki/Law_review, accessed on Oct. 10, 2016.

26. Law Review—Wikipedia, the free encyclopedia, http://en.wikipedia .org/wiki/Law_review, accessed on Oct. 10, 2016.

Chapter 2

1. In *Becoming a Law Professor, Part 1*, Anayat Durrani stated that "Law review is part of the resume of most candidates who are competitive on the teaching market." Anayat Durrani, *Becoming a Law Professor, Part 1*, accessed at www.lawcrossing.com on Oct. 11, 2016.

2. For a small number of students, there may be valid reasons not to join the law review. President Bill Clinton, while a student at Yale Law School, told a classmate of his he was not interested in joining the Yale Law Journal because it would not help him in politics in Arkansas. See Bill Clinton, My Life (2004). On the other hand, another law student who would go on to become a U.S. President, Barack Obama, served on the Harvard Law Review and was elected its president. His election as the first African American president of the Harvard Law Review was covered by the New York Times, landed him a lucrative book deal, and arguably gave him the platform to launch his political career in Illinois which resulted, ultimately, to his election as the nation's 44th President.

Chapter 3

1. Karen Hunter's blog, Reader Perspective, http://blogs.courant.com/ news_opinion_hunter/2016/01/uconn_law_schoo.html, accessed on May 17, 2016.

2. The San Diego Law Review's membership webpage, http:// www.sandiego.edu/law/academics/journals/sdlr, accessed on Dec. 8, 2016.

3. The Suffolk University Law Review's membership webpage, http:// suffolklawreview.org, accessed on Dec. 8, 2016.

4. The University of Miami Law Review's membership webpage, http:// lawreview.law.miami.edu/, accessed on Oct. 12, 2016.

5. The University of Chicago Law Review's membership webpage, http:// lawreview.uchicago.edu/, accessed on Oct. 12, 2016.

6. The California Law Review's webpage, http://californialawreview.org, accessed on Oct. 12, 2016.

7. The New York University Law Review's membership selection criteria webpage, http:/nyulawreview.org, accessed on Oct. 12, 2016.

8. The Harvard Law Review's membership webpage, http://harvardlaw review.org/, accessed on Nov. 22, 2016.

9. The California Law Review's webpage, http://californialawreview.org, accessed on Nov. 22, 2016.

10. The Washington Law Review's membership webpage, http://www.law .uw.edu/WLR/, accessed on Oct. 12, 2016.

11. The Illinois Law Review's membership webpage, http://illinois lawreview.org, accessed on Nov. 22, 2016.

Chapter 4

1. The George Washington University Law Review's webpage, http:// www.gwlr.org, accessed on Oct. 12, 2016.

2. The New York University Law Review's webpage, http://www.nyu lawreview.org, accessed on Oct. 12, 2016.1.

3. See generally Elizabeth Fajans & Mary R. Falk, *Scholarly Writing for Law Students: Seminar Papers, Law Review Notes and Law Review Competition Papers* 4–12 (4th ed. 2011).

4. Elizabeth Fajans & Mary R. Falk, *Scholarly Writing for Law Students: Seminar Papers, Law Review Notes and Law Review Competition Papers* 5 (4th ed. 2011).

5. Elizabeth Fajans & Mary R. Falk, *Scholarly Writing for Law Students: Seminar Papers, Law Review Notes and Law Review Competition Papers* 5 (4th ed. 2011).

6. Elizabeth Fajans & Mary R. Falk, *Scholarly Writing for Law Students: Seminar Papers, Law Review Notes and Law Review Competition Papers* 5 (4th ed. 2011).

7. Elizabeth Fajans & Mary R. Falk, *Scholarly Writing for Law Students: Seminar Papers, Law Review Notes and Law Review Competition Papers* 9 (4th ed. 2011).

8. Elizabeth Fajans & Mary R. Falk, *Scholarly Writing for Law Students: Seminar Papers, Law Review Notes and Law Review Competition Papers* 9–10 (4th ed. 2011) (footnotes omitted).

9. Elizabeth Fajans & Mary R. Falk, *Scholarly Writing for Law Students: Seminar Papers, Law Review Notes and Law Review Competition Papers* 10 (4th ed. 2011).

10. Elizabeth Fajans & Mary R. Falk, *Scholarly Writing for Law Students: Seminar Papers, Law Review Notes and Law Review Competition Papers* 10 (4th ed. 2011).

11. Elizabeth Fajans & Mary R. Falk, *Scholarly Writing for Law Students: Seminar Papers, Law Review Notes and Law Review Competition Papers* 10 (4th ed. 2011).

12. Elizabeth Fajans & Mary R. Falk, *Scholarly Writing for Law Students: Seminar Papers, Law Review Notes and Law Review Competition Papers* 11 (4th ed. 2011).

13. Richard Delgado, *How to Write a Law Review Article*, 20 U.S.F. L. Rev. 445, 446–47 (1986).

14. Richard Delgado, *How to Write a Law Review Article*, 20 U.S.F. L. Rev. 445, 446–47 (1986).

15. Richard Delgado, *How to Write a Law Review Article*, 20 U.S.F. L. Rev. 445, 448 (1986); see also Elizabeth Fajans & Mary R. Falk, *Scholarly Writing for Law Students: Seminar Papers, Law Review Notes and Law Review Competition Papers* 7 (4th ed. 2011).

Chapter 5

1. For example: Wes Henricksen, *Abay v. Ashcroft: The Sixth Circuit's Baseless Expansion of INA § 101(a)(42)(A) Revealed a Gap in Asylum Law*, 80 Wash. L. Rev. 477, 493–95 (2005).

2. This is an excerpt from *Abay v. Ashcroft: The Sixth Circuit's Baseless Expansion of INA § 101(a)(42)(A) Revealed a Gap in Asylum Law*, 80 Wash. L. Rev. 477, 480–82 (2005), by Wes Henricksen.

Chapter 6

1. Letter from Mark Twain (Samuel L. Clemens) to George Bainton (Oct. 15, 1888), found at: http://www.bartleby.com/73/540.html (accessed on Nov. 16, 2016).

2. Georgetown Law Center, Write On Sample Materials, https://www.law.georgetown.edu/academics/law-journals/writeon/samples.cfm (Nov. 3, 2016).

3. Ursula K. Le Guin, *Steering the Craft: Exercises and Discussions on Story Writing for the Lone Navigator or the Mutinous Crew* 19 (1998).

4. A more comprehensive list of transition words and phrases particularly applicable to legal writing can be found in Bryan Garner's book: *Legal Writing in Plain English: A Text with Exercises* 86 (2d ed. 2013). My list is an abbreviated version of the list compiled by Bryan Garner.

Afterword

1. These include, interestingly, the law libraries at Harvard, Stanford, and Yale, the first two of which denied my application when I applied to law school, and the last of which I did not even bother applying to; I knew I had no chance at Yale. The irony amuses me: my book has been warmly welcomed into numerous elite institutions that I, myself, was never allowed to step foot in.

2. Law School 411: Books & Films on Law & Law School, Excelling in Law School, found at: http://libguides.nyls.edu/content.php?pid=254648&sid=2102434 (Nov. 6, 2016).

3. You Can Do It : Guides to Making the Most of Law School, found at: https://law.wisc.edu/news/Law_Library_and_IT/You_Can_Do_It_Guides_to_Making_t_2009-10-29 (Feb. 22, 2016).

4. Law Review Write-On Competition: Recommended Resources, found at: http://sites.utexas.edu/Tarlton-library-news/2012/04/law-review-write-on-competition-recommended-resources/ (Nov. 6, 2016).

5. G. Tanner, There's no secret to write on competitions, Amazon.com, found at: http://www.amazon.com/Making-Law-Review-Write-Competition/dp/1594605203/ (Feb. 22, 2016).

6. Harry Dixon, Essential reading for anyone serious about the write-on competition, Amazon.com, found at: http://www.amazon.com/Making-Law-Review-Write-Competition/product-reviews/1594605203/ (Feb. 23, 2016).

Index

Names of law reviews and titles of books are in italic font.

A

admissions process, law review membership and, 27
aesthetics, in paper submissions, 82–85
  body text, footnotes/endnotes and, 84
  document format, 83–84
  headings, 84
  importance of, 82–83
  printing, 85
  reviewing old submissions for, 51
Alaska Law Review, 12–13
Alberta Law Review, 11
ALWD Citation Manual, 42 *box*
associate editors, 8
asylum under INA, casenote excerpt on, 48–50
Australia, law reviews in, 12
authorities, in submission papers
  claim selection and, 59
  inapplicable authorities, 61–62
  non-binding authorities, 62 *box*
  style/structure of, 81

B

Barry Law Review, 105 n.1
Becoming a Law Professor (Durrani), 107 n.1

benefits, from law review membership, 16–21
  acceptable credential for conversation, 17–18, 105 n.1
  employment opportunities, 16–17
  publishing opportunity, 19–20, 20 *box*
  relationship building, 18–19
  résumé building, 20–21
  skills building, 19
bluebooking proficiency
  Bluebook, knowledge of, 41–42, 79, 90
  Bluebooking quiz, 45–46, 101–104
  common errors, 43–45
  on footnotes/endnotes, 80
  on quotes, 80
  on signals, 81
  style manuals, knowledge of, 42 *box,* 46 *box*

C

California Law Review, 27, 28
California Style Manual, 42 *box*
Canada, law reviews in, 11–12
"case cruncher" article category, 35
casenotes, in write-on competitions, 33–34

casenote excerpt (*Washington Law Review*), 47–51
definitions, 33
old submission papers, using, 47
published student casenotes/comments, using, 47
claim selection
  best supported, by source materials, 59
  "it depends" argument, 60
  originality in, 59–60
  political bias in, 59–60
  prior knowledge, provided source materials and, 59
  prompts, issue selection and, 58, 60 *box*
Clinton, Bill, on law review membership, 107 n.2
Columbia Law Review, 9
comments, in write-on competitions, 34–36
  categories of, 35–36
  definitions, 33
  published student casenotes and comments, using, 47–51
"The Common Law Origins of the Infield Fly Rule" (*University of Pennsylvania Law Review*), 12
comparative law article category, 36
"A Compendium of Clever and Amusing Law Review Writings" (*Drake Law Review*), 12
composite-on, to law review, 27–28
Connecticut Law Review, 26
credit, academic *vs.* extracurricular, 9

D

Delgado, Richard (Professor), 34–36
dialogues continuing existing debates (article category), 35

discussions of legal profession, language, arguments (article category), 35
Dixon, Harry, 98
Drake Law Review, 12
drawbacks, to law review membership, 21–24
  peer backlash, 24
  relationship challenging, 22
  tedious duties, 22–23
  theoretical/obscure legal work, 23–24
  time consuming, 21–22, 21 *box*
Durrani, Anayat (*Becoming a Law Professor*), 107 n.1

E

editing exercises, 36, 87–90. *See also* bluebooking proficiency
  Bluebook use in, 90
  complacency, 89
  on computers, 88
  errors, in footnotes, 88–89
  instructions, 87
  note insertion, 89
  on paper, 87–88
  timing of, 71–72
editors, responsibilities of, 8
The Elements of Style (Strunk & White), 46 *box*
empirical research article category, 36

F

first draft papers, 60–71. *See also* editing exercises; organization, of personal statements; submission papers
  authorities, 61–62, 62 *box*
  concreteness, in words and phrases, 67–68
  counterarguments, 70

footnotes/endnotes, citations
     and, 63
headings, 64
humor and sarcasm in, 70
improve uniformity/flow, by
     reading aloud, 68–69, 73
instructions, 32, 61
page limits, 32, 71
paragraphs, sentence length
     and, 63–64
political bias in, 69–70
term selection, 67
voice, 65
word choice, importance of, 66
writing goal, 60–61
first year law students
grading-on, to law review, 25–26
legal writing course documents,
     using, 51
One-L write-on competition,
     15, 31
schedule challenges, 40–41
friends/family members, scheduling
     challenges for, 22, 41

G

George Washington Law Review, 11,
     32
grading-on (to law review), 25–26
grammar. *See* instructions; organi-
     zation, of submission papers;
     proofreading
Griswold, Edwin N. (Professor), on
     Harvard Law Review, 9

H

*Harvard Environmental Law Re-
     view,* 7
Harvard Law Review, 9, 28, 107 n.2
Holmes, Oliver Wendell, Jr.
     (Supreme Court Justice), on
     law reviews, 9

I

Illinois Law Review, 28
instructions, for write-on competi-
     tions, 32, 54–56
for editing exercises, 87
for first draft papers, 32, 61, 82
     box
mid-competition reminder, 72
     box
for personal statements, 91
prompt, 55–56
interdisciplinary article category, 35
IRAC, in submission papers, 81

L

law reform article category, 35
law review. *See also* membership
author's history on, 4–6
function of, 7
history of, 9–11
humor of, 12–13
law journal *vs.,* definitions, 7 *box*
managing/editing of, 7–8
statistics, 10–11, 10 *illus.*
U.S. Supreme Court cites of,
     23–24
law review informational meeting,
     39–40
law reviews
Alaska Law Review, 12–13
Alberta Law Review, 11
Barry Law Review, 105 n.1
California Law Review, 27, 28
Columbia Law Review, 9
Connecticut Law Review, 26
Drake Law Review, 12
"flagship" journals, 7
George Washington Law Review,
     11, 32
*Harvard Environmental Law Re-
     view,* 7

Harvard Law Review, 9, 28, 107 n.2
Holmes, Oliver Wendell, Jr. (Supreme Court Justice) on, 9
Illinois Law Review, 28
McGill Law Journal, 11
Melbourne Journal of International Law, 12
Melbourne University Law Review, 12
Michigan Law Review, 8, 9
Minnesota Law Review, 10–11
New York University Law Review, 27, 32
Northwestern University Law Review, 7, 23–24
Osgoode Hall Law Journal, 11
Revue de droit de McGill, 11
San Diego Law Review, 26
specialty law journals, 7, 10, 11, 12, 25
Suffolk University Law Review, 9, 26
Sydney Law Review, 12
Texas Journal of Women and the Law, 7
UCLA Law Review, 7
University of British Columbia Law Review, 11
University of Chicago Law Review, 26
University of Miami Law Review, 26
University of Pennsylvania Law Review, 9, 12
University of Toronto Faculty of Law Review, 11
Wake Forest Law Review, 13
Washington Law Review, 8, 28
Washington Law Review, casenote excerpt from, 47–51

"*Wiki Legal Journal,*" 13
Yale Journal of International Law, 7
Yale Law Journal, 9
The Lawyer Trip (McClurg), 13
Le Guin, Ursula K., on the sound of language, 68
legal history article category, 35
legalese, plain English *vs.,* 69
legislative notes (article category), 35
LSAT scores, membership and, 27, 39

M

main assignment, of write-on competitions, 31–32
Making Law Review (Henricksen), anecdotes from, 97–100
McClurg, Andrew J. ("The World's Greatest Law Review Article for Anyone Taking Life Too Seriously"), 13
McGill Law Journal, 11
Melbourne Journal of International Law, 12
Melbourne University Law Review, 12
membership, 25–29. *See also* benefits, from law review membership; drawbacks, to law review membership
composite-on, 27–28
grading-on, 25–26
noting-on, 28
responsibilities/opportunities of, 8–9
walking-on, 28–29
writing-on, 26–27
Michigan Law Review, 8, 9
Minnesota Law Review, 10–11

N

New York University (NYU) Law Review, 27, 32

Northwestern University Law Review, 7, 23–24
noting-on (to law review), 28

O

Obama, Barack, 107 n.2
1L of a Ride (McClurg), 13
1Ls. *See* first year law students
Order of the Coif, 22
organization, of submission papers, 72–78
  consistency, of argument, 76
  deleted material, 78
  importance of, 72–73
  improve uniformity/flow, by reading aloud, 73
  introductions, conclusions and, 78
  page limits, 32, 77–78
  paragraphs, topic sentences and, 74–76, 75 *box*
  redundancy, 76–77
  transition words/phrases, 75–76
Osgoode Hall Law Journal, 11

P

paper titles, in write-on competitions, 82
papers. *See* submission papers
personal schedule
  environment, importance of, 52–53
  long-range planning, 40–41
personal statements, 37, 91–93
  instructions, 91
  personal attributes/experiences, 92
  review of, by others, 93
  for specialty journals, 92–93
  writing/editing advice, 91–92
plain English, legalese *vs.,* 69
political bias, 59–60, 69–70

preparing, for write-on competitions, 39–52
  Bluebook, knowledge of, 41–46
  law review information meetings, 39–40
  long-range planning, 40–41
  style guides/manuals, knowledge of, 42 *box,* 46 *box*
  using previous submissions/notes and comments, 47–51
  using your first-year papers, 51
  writing atmosphere, 51–52
prompts, in instructions/claims, 55–56, 57, 58, 60 *box*
proofreading, 78–82, 85–86
  for basic grammar and punctuation errors, 78–79, 85
  citations, case names and, 79
  editing by others, 85–86, 93
  footnotes/endnotes, 80–81
  paper titles, 82, 82 *box*
  quotes, 80
  spell checking, 79 *box*
  style, structure and, 81

R

Reid, Joshua, 98
Revue de droit de McGill, 11

S

San Diego Law Review, 26
second-year editors, 8
source materials, 32, 56–58
  irrelevant sources, creative use of, 58 *box*
  statutes, 57 *box*
specialty law journals, 7, 10, 11, 12, 25
  personal statements for, 92–93
staff members, 8
statutes, in source materials, 57 *box*

Strunk, William, Jr. (*The Elements of Style*)
submission papers, 53–86. *See also* editing exercises; personal statements
  aesthetics, importance of, 82–85
  casenotes *vs.* comments, 33–36
  claim, selection of, 58–60
  first draft, advice on writing, 60–71
  grading of, 32
  instructions, 54–56
  main assignment, 31–32
  organization of, 72–78
  prompt, 55–56
  proofreading, 78–82, 85–86
  review old submission papers, 51
  review published casenotes, 47
  source materials, 56–58
  timeline, 32, 53–54
Suffolk University Law Review, 9, 26
Supreme Court of Canada, 11
Sydney Law Review, 12

T

Texas Journal of Women and the Law, 7
theory-fitting article category, 35
Twain, Mark, on importance of word choice, 66

U

UCLA Law Review, 7

University of British Columbia Law Review, 11
University of Chicago Law Review, 26
University of Miami Law Review, 26
University of Pennsylvania Law Review, 9, 12
University of Toronto Faculty of Law Review, 11

W

Wake Forest Law Review, 13
walking-on (to law review), 28–29
Washington Law Review, 8, 28
  casenote excerpt from, 47–51
White, E.B. (*The Elements of Style*)
Wiki Legal Journal, 13
"The World's Greatest Law Review Article for Anyone Taking Life Too Seriously" (McClurg), 13
write-on competitions
  advice, from author, 95
  editing exercises, 87–90
  guidelines for, 31–37
  personal statements, 91–93
  preparing for, 39–52
  submission papers for, 53–86
writing-on (to law review), 26–27. *See also* write-on competitions

Y

Yale Journal of International Law, 7
Yale Law Journal, 9